We Were Not the Enemy

We Were Not the Enemy

Remembering the United States'
Latin-American Civilian Internment
Program of World War II

Heidi Gurcke Donald

iUniverse, Inc.
New York Lincoln Shanghai

We Were Not the Enemy
Remembering the United States' Latin-American Civilian Internment
Program of World War II

iUniverse books may be ordered through booksellers or by contacting:

iUniverse
2021 Pine Lake Road, Suite 100
Lincoln, NE 68512
www.iuniverse.com
1-800-Authors (1-800-288-4677)

Because of the dynamic nature of the Internet, any Web addresses or links contained in this book may have changed since publication and may no longer be valid.

The views expressed in this work are solely those of the author and do not necessarily reflect the views of the publisher, and the publisher hereby disclaims any responsibility for them.

ISBN: 978-0-595-39333-6 (pbk)
ISBN: 978-0-595-83730-4 (ebk)

Printed in the United States of America

For Ingrid and Karl,
Alexa and Ian, Todd and Beau

*From a moral standpoint ... every foreign policy or series of policies
must be judged both by its intentions and its consequences at home and abroad.*
—Ernest W. Lefever

*Time's glory is to calm contending kings,
To unmask falsehood, and bring truth to light.*
—Shakespeare

We Were Not The Enemy, is a fascinating look at a … little-known piece of American history and stands with Jeanne Wakatsuki Houston's *Farewell to Manzanar* as a testimony to how patriotism can … go awry.

Mary McCaslin, *Santa Cruz Sentinel*

We Were Not the Enemy, Heidi Gurcke Donald's moving memoir about her family's fate at the hands of the U.S. government during World War II, is a critical addition to internment literature. The story Donald tells—of blacklists, of her father's abduction from Costa Rica, of the family's eventual internment for over a year in Crystal City, Texas—is shocking and heart-wrenching. It is the story of Latin-American governments, eager to rid their countries of German and Japanese economic competition, conspiring with our own State Department. Despite the tragedy, it is a story not without heroes—not the least of whom is Starr Gurcke, who keeps her faith in her husband's innocence despite long, grueling interrogations by FBI and INS officials in Los Angeles. For historians, *We Were Not the Enemy* will stand as a shocking antecedent to our government's present policy of extreme rendition. For others, this gripping memoir will stand as a reminder of the heartache engendered by wartime fear and panic.

John Christgau
Enemies: World War II Alien Internment

By now, it is widely known that 110,000 Japanese Americans were interned in War Relocation Authority camps during World War II. What is less well-known is that thousands more Japanese Americans were classified as "enemy aliens" and interned in Department of Justice camps, along with thousands of German-American and Italian-American "enemy aliens."

What is almost completely unknown is that the United States government, in violation of international law, collaborated with the governments of more than fifteen Latin-American countries to carry out a third program under which more than six thousand Latin Americans of German, Japanese, and Italian ancestry were deported from Latin America and interned in those same Department of Justice camps. These individuals included both resident immigrants and citizens of the countries from which they were deported.

Heidi Gurcke Donald's family was among those who, with little or no evidence and no legal procedures, were forced from their homes and shipped to the United States. In some ways, they were the lucky ones: partly because Heidi's mother was a U.S. citizen, they were allowed to leave the internment camp for "internment at large," and they were not "repatriated" to Germany in a prisoner exchange, as happened to many others.

This is a cautionary tale. It is a chapter of American history that is not taught in school. But it happened. And it could happen again, if we do not vigilantly safeguard our civil liberties.

Jay Feldman
When the Mississippi Ran Backwards
Suitcase Sefton and the American Dream

TABLE OF CONTENTS

ACKNOWLEDGMENTS

Thank you, *danke schön*, and *muchas gracias* to those family members, friends, and neighbors in Costa Rica and the United States who had the courage to look beyond the label of "enemy" during World War II, see us clearly, and help however and whenever possible.

My gratitude to Max Paul Friedman, who responded promptly and with kindness to all my requests for information about the German Latin-American experience. Art Jacobs—like me, a former Crystal City Camp kid—helped with my first attempts to access my parents' records. Jay Feldman, who is researching the era for a book of his own, read a draft of my memoir and graciously offered suggestions that improved it. Carol Fuller's interest in the Latin-American internment program and her efforts to educate a wider audience convinced me that this story was worth publication. Librarians at all levels, from my local library to the National Archives, deserve special thanks; they helped me ferret out information, even when my requests were imprecise and incomplete.

John Christgau was the first author to describe the consequences of the Alien Enemy Control program in his book, *Enemies: World War II Alien Internment* (recently republished as *Enemies*). Grace Shimizu directs the Japanese Peruvian Oral History Project and works tirelessly on behalf of former internees. Karen Ebel, a founding member of the German American Internee Coalition, is the national coordinator of efforts to achieve federal legislative recognition of the internment of German Americans and Latin Americans during World War II. John, Grace, and Karen have the facts at their fingertips, a fierce determination to get our stories out, and a shared concern for the families affected that is deeply inspiring.

Bruce, you knew and loved my parents, understood my preoccupation with this story, and have uncomplainingly weathered my neglect while I pursued it. Thank you.

PREFACE

I am in nursery school, and we are playing a singing game. Sleeping Beauty lies in the center of our circle, giggling as she tries to keep still, and we crouch around her. Sometimes my little sister or I get to be Sleeping Beauty, but usually we are part of the circle. We sing the verses and gradually stand taller, until finally we are all on tiptoe, hands held high over our heads, shouting the last verse—"The hedge grows very high!"—as we try to form an impenetrable barrier. A prince, chosen from the class, always gets through our hedge and frees our captive.

Our nursery school is surrounded by a different sort of hedge; the thorns are barbed wire. There are watchtowers and armed guards. There is no prince.

When I began looking into my family's imprisonment in World War II, my idea was to record what had happened for my children. As I learned more, I realized our experiences did not represent an isolated injustice to one family, but a pattern that occurs whenever a nation feels threatened. Families around the world are at risk whenever government policy-makers assume that ethnicity alone decides loyalty. I hope this look at an almost-unknown chapter of United States history will be a reminder that there are lessons to be learned from our past.

A number of thoroughly researched, well-written books are available on the World War II internment of civilians from the United States. For readers interested in a more comprehensive account of U.S. involvement in the southern hemisphere, I recommend Max Paul Friedman's *Nazis and Good Neighbors: The United States Campaign Against the Germans of Latin America in World War II*; and Leslie B. Rout Jr. and John F. Bratzel's *The Shadow War: German Espionage and United States Counterespionage in Latin America During World War II*. Stephen Fox's *Fear Itself: Inside the FBI Roundup of German Americans during World War II* and the German American Internee Coalition Web site, www.gaic.info, are also good sources of information.

INTRODUCTION

The United States implemented three programs to identify and imprison civilians considered a threat to the country during the war years. In all three, both legal resident aliens and naturalized citizens whose ethnicity was suspect were targeted, as were their families. Under the War Relocation Authority (WRA)—based on Executive Order 9066 (issued February 19, 1942)—all German, Japanese, and Italian enemy aliens were asked to voluntarily relocate from zones that the U.S. Army felt were militarily sensitive. Soon the request became a command for all Japanese, while only selected German and Italian aliens were ordered to move.[1]

The end result was the forcible mass uprooting and detaining, in "relocation camps," of most Japanese-American citizens and Japanese residing legally in the western states of California, Washington, and Oregon. Neither German nor Italian aliens were imprisoned under this program. No attempts were made to evaluate the risk individuals might pose.

Clearly, racial bias and overzealous security concerns motivated this policy. The United States recognized this in 1988, when all individuals affected by the WRA received a formal apology from Ronald Reagan; and in 1990, when each received $20,000 as redress.[2]

Somewhat more selectively, the Alien Enemy Control Unit, using the Alien Enemies Act of 1798, *did* attempt to evaluate and classify the potential dangers of individual Germans, Italians, and Japanese legally residing in the United States. However, evaluations were often perfunctory and inaccurate—based on reports of the Federal Bureau of Investigation (FBI) using information gleaned from neighbors, business associates, and family members.[3] Individuals and families picked up in this Department of Justice program were housed in camps run by the Immigration and Naturalization Service (INS). Out of a population of approximately 300,000 German Americans and legal German residents, around one percent were arrested and interned, many with their wives and children. In numerous cases, family members were U.S. citizens.[4] The Alien Enemies Act is still in use, most recently in the current "war on terror."

In a third, separate program, run by the State Department, at least 8,500 German nationals and numerous other Axis residents in Latin-American countries were indiscriminately swept into local detention centers. An unknown number were sent by the United States directly to Germany, Japan, or Italy, while 4,058

Germans, 2,264 Japanese, and 287 Italians were deported to the United States.[5] Again, some of the prisoners and many of their family members were citizens of the country from which they were expelled. These captives were also housed in the INS camps. The Axis nationals from Latin America and their families, though civilians, were treated with the standards used for prisoners of war, in the hope that Axis countries holding U.S. prisoners would reciprocate.[6] Under this program, which came to be called the Special War Problems Division, arrests and illegal deportations were so secret that the public knows little about it to this day.

The prime motive for these measures was to ensure hemispheric security, but commercial concerns were also incentives. Germans, in particular, had built up large businesses in Latin America. Destroying the businesses through blacklists and removing the German owners allowed U.S. firms to establish themselves. A third motive emerged as arrests and deportations continued, when government officials recognized that those interned could be exchanged for U.S. civilians imprisoned in Germany or Japan.

For readers interested in a broader look at the history behind United States policies toward citizen internment in Latin America prior to and during World War II, I have added a separate chapter, "A Wider View," at the end of this text, as well as a selected bibliography.

My family was one of many caught in the far-flung net cast by U.S. authorities seeking the enemy in Latin America during World War II. My father and uncle, Werner Gurcke and Karl Oskar Gurcke, were German citizens who had lived in Costa Rica since the 1920s. In the early 1930s, Karl Oskar married a Costa Rican woman with one young daughter. In 1936, my father married an American— Starr Pait, my mother—and they made their home in the capital, San José, where my sister and I were born. Blacklisted by the British in August 1940 and the United States in 1941, my father and uncle were arrested as Nazis and dangerous enemy aliens in 1942 and held without charges for six months. Then both our families were deported to the United States and interned in a camp at Crystal City, Texas.

Was my father a Nazi? Absolutely not. In January 1942, when my father registered as a resident alien in Costa Rica, he made clear that he was not at all interested in politics, preferring to concentrate on family and business. Letters both my parents wrote during the war years indicated strong dislike for Nazi policies. A governmental review of my father's case in 1946 concluded there was no evidence he even tacitly sympathized with Hitler's aims. Our family's whole ordeal hinged on unsubstantiated allegations by anonymous informants—and one fact; my father was born in Germany.

In several letters, both my father and mother stated that other members of his family *did* have Nazi leanings. I have no evidence that any of them belonged to the Nazi Party, although they may have been nationalistic. Because my uncle and his family chose to be sent to Germany, no U.S. government review of his case was ever done.

In 1946, my father's status as alien enemy was finally dropped, after he received the first full hearing and review of his case, but charges of illegal entry into the United States threatened repatriation until 1948. From 1940, when my parents were blacklisted in Costa Rica, until the day my father became a citizen of the United States on April 21, 1952, my parents lived with uncertainty and fear. If they had realized that even naturalized U.S. citizenship would not have safeguarded my father during the war years, they would never have felt secure again.

I learned part of our story from my mother, who was in her eighties when she finally let me interview her. Her memories were so painful that it took over a month of visits to record her recollections, offered in fragments through her tears. My father never talked about any of it. He had faced not only the destruction of his own way of life, but also the distress of knowing his parents and youngest brother were living through another war in Germany. After his death, I found he'd saved numerous letters and governmental papers, tucking them into a shabby manila folder at the back of an old filing cabinet in the garage.

Other documents and information were obtained through Freedom of Information and Privacy Act requests to various government agencies. I have not altered the abbreviated spellings my mother often used in her letters. All translations are my own. (Book revised and updated, 2008.)

"Introduction" Endnotes

[1] Tetsuden Kashima, *Judgment Without Trial: Japanese American Imprisonment During World War II* (Seattle: University of Washington Press, 2003), 136–139.

[2] See Commission on Wartime Relocation and Internment of Civilians, *Personal Justice Denied* (Seattle: The Civil Liberties Public Education Fund and the University of Washington Press, 1997); Max Paul Friedman, *Nazis and Good Neighbors: The United States Campaign Against the Germans of Latin America in World War II* (New York: Cambridge University Press, 2003); and Michi Weglyn, *Years of Infamy: The Untold Story of America's Concentration Camps* (Seattle: University of Washington Press, 1996). Japanese- and Italian-American groups affected by WWII internment policies have had governmental recognition. The apology and $20,000 given to Japanese Americans in the War Relocation Authority program were also extended to Japanese Americans interned by Alien Enemy Control. In 2000, a law was enacted authorizing a government report detailing injustices suffered by Italian Americans during World War II. The president signed a formal admission of these injustices. No acknowledgment has been made to civilians of German ancestry who experienced similar treatment.

[3] Arnold Krammer, *Undue Process: The Untold Story of America's German Alien Internees* (Maryland: Rowman and Littlefield Publishers Inc., 1997), 11.

[4] Friedman, *Nazis and Good Neighbors,* 3, 120. In total, 10,905 Germans were interned, including those brought to the United States and voluntary internees, according to a letter from W. F. Kelly to A. Vulliet, 9 August 1948, which was reprinted in *The World War Two Experience: The Internment of German-Americans, Vol. IV, German-Americans in the World Wars,* Arthur D. Jacobs and Joseph E. Fallon, eds. (Munich: K. G. Saur, 1996), 1513.

[5] White to Lafoon, January 1946, "Statistics," Subject Files 1939–54, Box 70, Special War Problems Division, RG 59 (National Archives, College Park, Maryland).

[6] See Edward N. Barnhart, "Japanese Internees from Peru," *Pacific Historical Review* 31 (1962): 172. See also Max Paul Friedman, *Personal Justice Denied;* "Private Memory, Public Record, and Contested Terrain: Weighing Oral Testimony in the Deportation of Germans from Latin America During World War II," *Oral History Review* 27/1 (Winter/Spring 2000); and Friedman, *Nazis and Good Neighbors,* 2–3. In 1998, President Bill Clinton offered a public apology and agreed to pay $5,000 compensation to Peruvian Japanese, but no formal acknowledgment of similar injustices to Latin-American Germans and Italians has been made. In June 1942, the United States also ordered the evacuation of residents of the Aleutian and Pribiloff Islands in Alaska, as a precaution to ensure their safety during Japanese attacks on some of the islands. While not part of the prior programs, these people likewise suffered great losses economically and personally. Their story is told in *Personal Justice Denied.*

First Impressions

Two small albums of black-and-white photographs and a thin handful of old letters written by my parents are my only clues to their first years together. We children knew the story of how they met; when I was younger, I thought it terribly romantic. In 1934, Starr—who was to become my mother—was traveling to Munich, Germany, to begin a postgraduate year of Germanic language studies. When her ship docked in Hamburg, Werner, my father-to-be, came to meet his uncle, one of Starr's shipboard acquaintances. Her knowledge of German was immediately put to the test, because the three of them had coffee at the Alster Pavilion together. Over the next several days, Starr and Werner spent time alone with each other. He was visiting his family but would soon return to Central America, where he made his home.

In the brief few days of their first meeting, the handsome, rangy young German and his account of life in Costa Rica enchanted Starr. She had never even heard of Costa Rica before. How they talked! As they walked along the Alster, he told her stories of jungles full of orchids and colorful birds; of the smell of coffee flowers in the rain; of smoking volcanoes; and of wild, untamed rivers. He described the capital city of San José, where he had his business; spoke about his friends; and told her about his brother, who lived many miles away on a cattle ranch.

They laughed at the coincidence of living in San José—she in California, he in Costa Rica. He listened intently as she told him that after graduating from San Jose State, she cared for her mother, who was suffering a series of strokes. When her mother died in 1933, Starr returned to school, received a master's degree from Stanford University just that past July, and then caught the boat for Germany.

While Starr went on to school, he returned to Costa Rica. They must have written to each other, but she saved only one rather formally written postcard from him.

Then Starr became ill with glandular tuberculosis and was forced to drop out of school, while hospitalized in a sanatorium. Recovered after several months of treatment, she returned home in the summer of 1935, driving across the country from New York with a fellow American student from Munich. The pair visited his family at their farm in the Midwest and then continued to California. It was great fun roaring along the road, convertible top down. But when he became serious, asking her to marry him, she refused; instead she returned to live quietly alone in the Santa Cruz beach house that she and her brother, Charles, inherited after their mother's death.

1

That Christmas, Werner came to visit. He was charming, gentle, and earnest. His stories of life in Central America seemed so fascinating and thrilling that when he proposed on Christmas Eve, she said yes immediately. They married as soon as they were able—in mid-January—and then he left. While he'd had high hopes that they would marry, his optimism hadn't extended to the purchase of two boat passages for the return trip. She was to follow as soon as she could.

In March 1936, Starr boarded a freighter bound for Costa Rica with her newly acquired cocker spaniel puppy, Sudi, and a trunk full of possessions. She must have been both excited and nervous about meeting the man she had married after such a brief courtship. Werner greeted her when the ship docked in Puntarenas, the Pacific coast port. Then they traveled by train to San José, the capital of Costa Rica, where Werner had his business—and where he'd rented a home for the two of them.

Three months after her arrival, Starr sat down to write a letter to Liz, a friend from California whom she'd known since her first day of high school. Starr had been only ten. Liz, though older, befriended her immediately, and they were inseparable through much of the next four years. (It was fashionable in those days to encourage bright students to skip grades. My mother's family allowed her to skip at least two. She told me she had been a very young ten-year-old, and so unhappy at first she brought her favorite doll to classes. I suspect that Liz may have been one of the few students who was kind and didn't tease her.) While Starr wrote to numerous friends, only Liz saved the letters and eventually returned them.

Starr with Sudi on shipboard, departing for Costa Rica

... Werner gets off to the office about 8:00, walks to town (about 15 minutes) and leaves me at the mercy of the Spanish jabbering girl. I was terrified at first and ran around all day looking up words in the dictionary of things to eat and work to do, but now we get along beautifully; she understands my few words and gestures and speaks very slowly for me.

My mornings are usually spent doing the shopping for the day (gardeners come by the door all morning with fruits and vegetables and such like), planning the meals, seeing that the house is clean, watering my plants (I'm making a collection of queer tropical plants), working in the garden, studying Spanish, etc.... Afternoons I take a Spanish lesson ... go to a movie, go visiting, then at 5 go to meet Werner at the office to walk home ... Evenings we usually simply sit and listen to the radio, which we got 2 days ago.... It's a grand one, we can get practically all the world.... How's that for a lazy life?

My husband is a terrificly energetic person, I'm discovering. He works hard all week long, then Sundays always takes me touring the country on a picnic over the awfullest roads and thru rivers and up mountains, til I ache all over from being bumped around. Then we get out and hike til my legs won't work any more, thru pouring rain or in the hottest heat, but it's lots of fun. And just about every Sunday we gather new, strange-looking plants and flowers and ferns to bring home and establish here. It's an old Spanish custom to have plants all over your house, ... and I'm trying to look Spanish.

Driving was circumscribed even in good weather, with only about one hundred kilometers (around sixty-two miles) of paved and semipaved road to the east and west of San José. There was a train to Limón on the Atlantic coast and Puntarenas on the Pacific, but those journeys were long, slow, hot, and dirty. Extensive trips elsewhere, like to Guatemala or Panama, could only be made by boat, which was very expensive and took time to arrange. Horseback, river-launch, small airplane, or on foot were the only ways to get around much of the country. Because Werner had decided they would spend Christmas at his brother's ranch, which could only be reached on horseback, he was giving Starr riding lessons.

Twice we've been horseback riding, the first time, my first experience on a horse, only a short way while I yelled and screamed to Werner to go slow who didn't pay the slightest attention to me. I galloped off at a great speed and scared myself to death. The second time we went dove hunting. Werner got me up at 5 o'clock in the morning and [we] rode ... up a high mountain thru dripping coffee and banana trees and a fog so thick you couldn't see where your horse was going. We went with another young couple and the other wife and I were left to sit, shivering in the fog and rain for hours until the men got back—without a single dove!

How she must have hated that day. There wasn't a trace of a smile as she posed for a picture, sitting on the soaked grass with a shotgun across her knees.

The outdoor life of Costa Rica is really grand, the best part of it. It's a perfectly beautiful country, all mountains and junglish forest and rivers, and covered with peculiar vegetation, tropical ferns, simply huge, and hanging plants and banana trees and coffee and sugar cane. Unfortunately the rainy season is beginning in earnest now and it rains regularly every afternoon in bucketsful. Mornings and evenings are usually beautiful and clear. But the rains make most of the roads so bad that it's impossible to get off the main highways which aren't as numerous as they might be here.... The rains last until about

Starr, Costa Rica 1936

November, then summer starts when it's supposed to be cooler.

... The house where we're living is like most Costa Rican houses which isn't saying much, but much newer and better equipped than most ... In spite of a large city with movies and 1 good hotel and street cars and automobiles and all the ear marks of civilization, there are still lots of primitive conditions here that make a spoiled American used to electric appliances and modernities and canned goods, squirm and wish for a Piggly-Wiggly or Woolworth store.

... One thing we have that's a real rarity here is a big, modern, white, clean bathroom with shower and tile floor. I haven't seen another one like it.... Then soon we're to get from Germany a small electric stove with oven which I'm looking forward to. Up to now we've had only small, single electric burners and no oven, which is the general thing here.

People take Society with a capital S here very seriously. In a small country with only one city and that about as big as S.J. [San Jose], California, and with certain definite cliques, everyone knows everyone else and what he does and what he says and wears, etc. We "belong" to the German colony which is pretty large and also have friends in the American clique and a few native Costa Ricans. There's a German Club with Club House where the Germans gather; there are lots of social goings-on chiefly because of the lack of other amusements. Other people don't seem to find a life of quiet and being alone as entertaining as Werner and I do, so they're constantly giving teas and dances and parties of all sorts. For a while to get me introduced and properly displayed in the best places, Werner took me around to peoples' houses ... until I was fed up with it.

There are lots of movies here but only 3 where the "best" people go (that is, where the sound apparatus is any good), there's 1 good, modern, elegant Hotel where you go to dance Saturdays and Sunday nites and to drink coffee and cocktails, there's one worthwhile restaurant when you want to eat out, there are 3 or 4 respectable places to drink beer, there's the German Club, where you swim and play tennis and dance or simply sit and talk—outside of these places there's no place to go and nothing to do.

Starr and Werner at the German Club pool, 1936

But for some crazy reason in spite of this apparent lack of amusement and having my work all done for me, the days aren't long enuf to do all the things I want to do and the time fairly seems to fly. I can't believe it's actually been three months since I arrived, 3 months yesterday.

Have I given you the impression that it's a nice place to live or the reverse? Anyway I love it ... Please write me soon, Liz, and tell me about your affairs. Love, Starr

By September of that year, some of Starr's enthusiasm for the foreignness of Costa Rica was fading. She was getting homesick. In fact, she so longed for the sound of English that she pestered Werner into beginning "English weeks," during which they would speak only English, not German or Spanish, to each other.

Since he knew only a few words, she became his tutor. As far as she was concerned, teaching him was very satisfactory. She was tired of being the only one who had to search for words and took slightly malicious delight in Werner's struggles to remember words or phrases. The rainy season had begun in earnest by then, curtailing their explorations of the countryside. And Starr was beginning to be nervous about an impending meeting with her new mother-in-law, Frieda Gurcke, who planned to come from Hamburg to spend three months in Costa Rica. In another letter, Starr wrote,

> As a matter of fact, Liz, I'm not quite the lady of leisure you think I am or as I may seem at a casual glance.... You see, this servant business isn't everything it's cracked up to be, I'm slowly finding out. I'm a lady of leisure but with a worried look in my eye. I don't know how it happens but the girl works all day and never seems to get things done. I sort of have to keep urging and urging her on, please clean this, please do that, please wash, please iron and so on.
>
> ... Sometimes I actually envy you the privilege of being able to do your own work! Here it's simply an impossibility. For a week I tried it when the girl was sick and was really a nervous wreck. In the first place there aren't any of the conveniences, the snappy, labor-saving devices, here as you have. There aren't any cute little kitchens with mix masters and toasters and running hot water and washing machines, etc. Labor is labor and you can't run to the corner Piggly Wiggly and get a can or two for supper. You go to the Market downtown twice a week and shop and buy everything in its natural state.
>
> Another work discouraging factor is the climate.... The altitude and warmth (I won't say heat, because for the tropics it's actually cold) makes you prefer to sit and do nothing most of the time. So you see it's not as ideal as it may sound ...
>
> Had I had my hair cut when I wrote last? I don't think so. Anyway I did and permanent waved! ... I was awfully disappointed at first and Werner said I looked like the Bride of Frankenstein (did you see that movie?). But I soon got it under control and ... it's so much easier to care of....
>
> My riding isn't progressing very much. I've only been twice on horseback, but it's been raining so much and the roads are all so wet and muddy that it's been almost impossible. This Sunday though, we're going to try it again. I'm still not much good, as you can imagine; I'm very nervous and ride at a nice slow walk, but I'm anxious to get better before Christmas. Then we're going to Werner's brother's farm [near Tilaran, in Guanacaste], as I probly told you before, with their mother who is com-

ing from Germany sometime in November for a Christmas visit with her sons. Then we'll have to travel part way by airplane and part way by horseback. Heaven help poor Mrs. Gurcke and me, too, unless I improve mighty fast. But I'm sure we'll manage somehow if we have to walk beside the horses. It ought to be fun. The farm is in the midst of real junglish forests and is very primitive. I'm a little dubious about the comforts of home, but if Mrs. G. can stand it, I can.

Next Sunday … has a holiday the following Monday, so we're taking a weekend trip to Limón, the Atlantic port of Costa Rica, just to satisfy my curiosity. It's supposed to be very tropical and interesting and hot as Hell, and I'm looking forward to seeing it.… It's really not very far away from San José but takes 6 hours on the train, which is very small and stops at every tiny station …

Frieda Hickfang Gurcke arrived November 1 for an extended stay. Since she and Starr had never met, there was an initial awkwardness, soon replaced on Starr's side by frequent silent resentment. To begin with, Werner was a different person with his mother around. He seemed timid and unsure of himself, devoting much effort in trying to please her. Mrs. Gurcke, on the other hand, courted attention; most of their time was spent taking her on interminable visits to friends' and distant relatives' homes, where all the talk was about people Starr didn't know and events she hadn't been part of.

Then there were her mother-in-law's attempts to teach her "proper" housekeeping skills. Frieda, (whom Starr called "Mrs. G."), intervened constantly while Starr tried to instruct their new maid, Millicent, on household routines. It had been hard enough to sack Olga, the original maid, who had become complacent and simply didn't do what she didn't want to do—which was almost everything. At least Millicent spoke some English … but with Frieda's steady stream of suggestions—all in German—Starr could feel her teeth gritting, as she tried to stay pleasant and calm.

The arrival in early December of Werner's brother, Karl Oskar (nicknamed Ocki), his wife, Paulina Carlotta Vargas de Gurcke (known as Pany), and stepdaughter, Hermida Jinesta, added enormously to her stress. Native Costa Ricans, neither Starr's sister-in-law nor her new niece spoke German. That meant all conversations were a tangle of Spanish and German, and sometimes Starr simply couldn't find any words in any language. They stayed for two weeks, and she kept extremely busy seeing that everyone was well fed and, she hoped, happy. She was trying so hard to be a perfect hostess to all these people she'd never met before—especially to her mother-in-law—that she felt exhausted.

As soon as Ocki's family left for their ranch, it was time for Werner, Starr, and Frieda to get ready to join them for Christmas. Their ranch was an extremely primitive affair set far off in the northwestern mountains—not easy to get to. And Frieda brought a trunk full of Christmas *mitbringsels*, little presents that needed to be taken.

The trip was hellish. First, there was the hour-plus airplane trip—Starr's first—which was rough enough to make all of them airsick. They arrived in Cañas—a muddy, hot, tiny little town in the mountains—where they climbed on the horses they would ride for the next seven hours. It was stormy and raining, and they had to ford two rivers and ride on "awful, steep slippery trails," over four hours of the time in the dark.

On top of that, Starr wore slacks to ease her constant worry that she might fall off her horse and risk embarrassment. She hardly ever wore them, because she felt they made her look fat. By the time the travelers arrived at the ranch, she felt like an overstuffed sausage and was frantic to take off the wet wool encasing her and her painfully bruised behind.

on the way to Karl Oskar's cattle ranch, near Tilaran, in Guanacaste

Karl Oskar (left) and Werner at the ranch

Tilaran, Christmas 1936
from left: unknown child, Starr, Hermida,
Frieda, Pany
in back: Werner and Karl Oskar

Her bed "seemed like heaven" that night, hard as it was. And the next day, the travelers took baths in the river and washed out their mud-spattered clothes. There was no running water and no electricity, but Ocki and Pany had plentiful food and drink, and the presents that Frieda brought added a great deal to the "fiesta" spirit of the occasion. It *did* seem very strange to be celebrating Christmas during the pleasant, supposedly sunny season called summer in Costa Rica, with a group of near strangers. It was all so unusual that Starr had no time to be homesick.

And then—joy of joys!—she and Werni left alone, while Frieda spent the month of January at the ranch. The trip back was not as hard. The weather had improved, and they stayed overnight in a funny little hotel before taking the airplane home. And Werner seemed his old self again: calm, competent, and self-assured.

Their maid, Millicent, was celebrating the holidays with family, so Starr spent several days planning a very special dinner menu to celebrate Werner's twenty-eighth birthday on January 10. Starr had never been particularly interested in any of the practical arts of running a home; as a teenager and young adult, she read and daydreamed through the days, never learning to cook or sew.

She decided to make Werner a chocolate cake, using the recipe on the back of the cocoa container. Their new stove, with oven, had arrived from Germany, and she'd been practicing with it, mostly making cookies. She was also going to make a chicken pie—her first. Whether her attempts were completely successful, I don't know, but there is a picture of Werner smiling down at a birthday cake that looks quite presentable. Although that photo is my only clue, I can imagine what might have happened that day:

Werner is extremely pleased. He eats everything in sight and praises every bite. With Costa Rican dance music playing on the radio, Starr washes dishes while he dries. Dishes done, Werner suddenly becomes a wild-eyed German Don Juan, leering at his wife and stroking an imaginary mustache: "¡Ay, caramba!" Clutching her hand, he glides through the kitchen out to the living room, where they dip and twirl, more or less successfully avoiding the furniture, until they collapse, breathless and laughing on the big living-room couch. Sipping coffee laced with Grand Marnier, an orange liqueur they always saved for special occasions, he opens his presents.

How had my father and his brother come to live in Costa Rica, so far from their birthplace in Hamburg, Germany? I asked him once, many years ago, and this is what he told me.

World War I, the Great War (1914–18), began when he, Werner, was five. His father, Max, was an officer in the military and was often away from home, on duty. Werner, his mother, Frieda, and Karl Oskar (who was nine when the war began) lived by themselves, although many aunts and uncles on both sides of the family visited frequently.

Food soon became scarce, and he remembered that his mother made meals from rutabagas—often the only food available in quantity. She made stews flavored with a bit of ham bone and wild onions picked from the garden; she also baked bread of a sort, using rutabaga flour, and served it with a rutabaga jam when sugar was available. It seemed to him, looking back on his childhood, that he was always hungry; somewhere during those years, he acquired the nickname "Hollow Legs," based on his capacity to eat all that he was offered.

As the war dragged on, Frieda sent Ocki and Werner out to stand at street corners with buckets to collect horse manure, which their mother dried to use as fuel to heat their home. Werner told me that Karl Oskar treated this duty as beneath him, demanding that Werner fill both buckets and threatening him if he told.

After the war, inflation skyrocketed. Werner and Ocki took turns on Fridays—their father's payday—collecting their father's check at his workplace and running to the bank with it. Their mother would meet them there and immediately cash it. The family would then hurry to the store to buy as much as they could, while they could. By that time (1919), another son, Ülrich, had been born to the Gurckes.

Once, my father confessed, he saw a toy in a shop window that he coveted with all his heart. He noted the price, and when he got home, he begged and cajoled his father, who finally gave him the money. But by the next morning, when he raced joyfully to the store, the price of the toy had tripled. It was then, when he was ten or so, that he resolved to live where there was plenty of food and money—and no war—when he grew up.

Werner, Costa Rica, 1930's

Karl Oskar must have decided the same, because when he reached adulthood, he booked passage for Costa Rica. Costa Rica was distant but not unknown to the Gurckes. Relatives had moved there at the turn of the century and had kept in touch with Max and Frieda. One of them offered Karl Oskar work and would offer the same to Werner a few years later—when, at the age of twenty, he left Germany. My father still kept a clipping from the July 6, 1929, edition of a local newspaper, *La Nueva Prensa*, which noted his arrival.

One of our family photograph albums displays two pictures of Werner with his brother and father. In the first, Werner is a sweet-faced three or so, dressed in a knit sailor suit, wearing a felt hat with a jaunty feather. He rests one hand gently on his father's arm. In the second picture, Werner has grown. There are dark circles under his eyes, and he is somber. His hand clutches his father's sleeve so tightly the cloth bunches under his fingers.

At the end of January, Werner's mother returned from Karl Oskar's cattle ranch to spend another month with Starr and Werner. During that visit, Starr and Werner moved to a home on one of the nicest streets in San José.

April 7, 1937
Dear Liz:

… on Feb. 1 we moved, Mrs. Gurcke came back to stay with us and the girl doing the housework left us to shift for ourselves.… Believe me, that was a hectic time. Moving here is no snap; there are no nice big moving vans that take all your baggage away in one big swoop. You do most of it yourself and then hire a little truck to take big things in about 6 different trips. Then comes the settling down afterwards, making curtains, cleaning house, etc. etc. and, of course, in the one month left here for Mrs. G. there were people popping in at all hours to visit her and visits to be made on our part.

Werner and I felt we deserved a vacation, so when we went with his mother to Limón, the Atlantic port, to see her off on the boat, we stayed there a week and lazed about, having a grand time, sweating and going swimming and sweating some more. (I know perspiring is more elegant, but it's sweating you do in Limón.) ...

We now live on the oldest and most aristocratic residence street in C.R., but if we're not very careful and keep the front gate closed, the cows and horses that wander about loose, will insist on coming in to eat off our flowers and grass. From the front of the house the view is very citified—the street is paved and lined with sidewalks, flowering trees and a street car, very clean and orderly—but from the back we might be living a thousand miles from town. Beyond our yard, civilization ceases; you see only waving banana leaves, forested mountains and in the distance, a beautiful volcano.

... We also actually have a sink affair in the kitchen, oh, no—not a nice, big, beautiful white porcelan [sic] business with hot and cold running water, just a big stone construction with a little cold water faucet and a stone drainboard. The bathroom is a little peculiar, too. When you want a hot bath, you fill the tub, light a tiny heater under it and wait about 5 hours til the water's hot. Of course, with time the tub burns thru in the middle, but that's the landlady's worry, not ours. But one gets used to everything, I hear, so I'm not discouraged and the other, nice features of the house completely override the few bad ones....

I've at last attacked the mysteries of sewing on a German sewing-machine with a book of instructions in Spanish and successfully solved them. Not only have I made a few curtains already but have actually attempted making a dress for myself, which turned out better than my wildest dreams had imagined.... I'd always had the idea that dress-making was something that was only learned after years of practice and by very gifted people in the practical arts, which I am not. The impossibility of getting ready-made clothes here and cheapness and great variety of good material practically forced me to it ...

In May Starr received a letter from her brother, Charles Pait, asking when and how he and his wife, Virginia, could come for a visit. Delighted at the prospect of seeing them, Starr began to worry about how they were going to get there. From San Francisco, they'd have to take a boat through the Panama Canal, since no vessels stopped on the Pacific side when coffee wasn't being shipped. Then they had to get to Limón, on the Atlantic side, and from there take the train to San José.

By this time, she was truly homesick, wanting "to gossip as fast and furiously as possible" in her native language. She also longed for some of the labor-saving devices available in the States. A new living-room rug sent out "clouds of dust" even though she brushed it thoroughly every day for over a month. "Don't mention vacuum cleaners; I've never encountered one here.... I feel very much like a good old sturdy '49er woman, making bread, making all my own clothes, painting furniture etc. etc. I remind myself of my grandmother. I also put up fruit, marmalades, jams, jellies, etc. Maybe it's just because I've never done such things before nor gave them a thot, that I consider myself pioneerish."

Starr began to wake in the night, thinking about Costa Rica as she had first seen it. Would her brother and his wife like it here? You had to make friends with *cucarachas* (cockroaches), mosquitoes, fleas, ants, warm weather, lots of rain, cold showers, filth in the marketplace, static on the radio, bad roads, and so on. Of course, if Charles and Virginia stayed only a few months, she thought, vigorous use of a flit gun would help keep insects at bay. And she would get them a mosquito net so they could sleep in peace, at least.

In July, she received word that Charles and Virginia were on their way. Starr's brother and his wife celebrated their third wedding anniversary sailing out of San Francisco under the Golden Gate Bridge. Two weeks later they reached Panama, but were unable to find a boat to Limón, and ended up flying into San José.

The longed-for visit was a great success. Though touring was limited to paved roads because it was the rainy season, Starr and Werner showed their visitors what they could of Costa Rica. They spent a long weekend in Limón, where everyone swam and lounged on the beach. In San José, they went dancing at the hotel roof garden; saw all the movies being shown (*Lost Horizons*, *Romeo and Juliet*,

from left: Werner and Starr, Charles and Virginia
Limón, Costa Rica, 1937

and *Swing Time*); and attended a concert at the National Theater, which was (and still is) considered one of the most beautiful buildings in Costa Rica. There were trips to the orchid garden and the zoo. Charles, who was a medical student at Stanford University, visited the San José hospital, which Starr had been told was the most famous hospital in all Central America. And, of course, everyone talked and talked.

Starr was happy that Charles was able to spend time getting to know Werner. Werner spoke much better English than he had when Charles first met him, thanks to the "English weeks" he and Starr practiced each month. Discovering that "California isn't so terribly far away from here and can be reached in 10 days" reduced her feelings of homesickness and isolation temporarily.

After the Paits left, Starr and Werner settled back into a quieter life. Werner's business partner took an extended trip to Germany, which meant Werner had much more work to do. Starr kept busy with Spanish lessons, cooking, painting the interior of their new home, and sewing.

One rainy afternoon in October 1937, realizing it had been a long, long time since she'd written to Liz, Starr settled down at the dining table and began to recap Charles and Virginia's visit. When she finished, she wondered if she should tell Liz about the plague of bad luck she and Werner were having? Why not? Some of it was disgusting … but also interesting.

First, there was the bullfight; the grandstand they were sitting on collapsed with several hundred people on it. She and Werner escaped with only bad bruises and torn clothes, but it had been a horrible fright.

> Then I had to have an operation on the breast for a "*tárzalo*." Just wait til I explain what that is!! It's a fly that bites usually horses and cows, but also occasionally humans, lays its eggs in the flesh and moves on. The bite itches furiously, but looks like an ordinary mosquito bite until the eggs hatch and the *worm*, (yes, worm!) begins to develop and get hungry inside. Then he starts eating flesh, gets bigger, a protective fat tumor is built up by the body around him, he hurts like hell and can be seen sticking his head out of the hole in the wound for air. When I finally became aware of this beast in my breast of all places, I was practically sick with disgust. Well, he and the tumor had to be removed, and after some bad days, I recovered. Did you ever hear of anything so revolting? Altogether I nourished the animal in my bosom for about a month …

Starr had been hospitalized to have the parasite removed, and the surgery site was still sore when she wrote the letter. She went on to tell her friend about the theft of their car battery and the robber who'd run off with her gold watch, though these woes seemed anticlimactic compared to the worm from hell.

Starr and Werner, picnic in Costa Rica
1936 or 1937

Christmas 1937 was again spent with Karl Oskar and Pany in Guanacaste. Instead of flying, Starr and Werner took a train to Puntarenas one day. The next day, they rode a small launch out into the gulf and up the Río Bebedero to a little town of the same name. There they caught a bus to Cañas, where they picked up horses and rode the six-plus hours on horseback to the farm. Starr described the trip in a letter to Liz.

This "bus" ride of 2 hours or more was an experience never-to-be-forgotten! There is no road and these big old cars go tearing thru a complete wilderness, dodging trees and rocks, half turning over in some of the ruts.... There [were] lots of monkeys, ... big, white faced brutes that make a noise halfway between a scream and a roar. We bounced around on hard board seats till we were black and blue and picked leaves and branches of trees out of our hair and laps when we arrived.... The launch trip, tho, was perfectly beautiful, especially on the way home when we saw the river by dawn. We saw all sorts of tropical birds, huge cranes and these big squawking brilliantly-colored parrots, roaring Congo monkeys and 'iguanas', lizards that sleep in the trees overhanging the river....

Costa Rica *really* was as picturesque and exotic as Werner described it when he met Starr in Hamburg in 1934. He hadn't exaggerated at all.

THE NAZI SHADOW

In the early spring of 1938, German embassies and legations around the world sent notice to all known German citizens, ordering them to report April 8 for a referendum demanded by Adolf Hitler. He wanted to assess their approval of Nazi annexation of Austria and the strength of their support for his regime.

Because holding a German vote on foreign soil was impolitic to say the least, voters were to go to certain ports, so ships could take them out to international waters. Some countries, such as the United States, had such large numbers of German citizens that this plan for voting was impractical, and in some countries, signatures of support were gathered rather than real ballots.[1] In Costa Rica, a referendum was planned and ships procured.

When Werner brought the notice home, he was deeply disturbed. For the first time, he told Starr about an ugly incident that occurred when he was treasurer at the German Club. In November 1934, Herbert Knöhr, a local Nazi leader, invited Mr. Kuehn, an official of the Nazi Patrol in Panama, to address the club's board. The official demanded that the directors approve a Nazi Party takeover of the club. Werner, the president, and other directors were highly opposed. Mr. Kuehn was furious and hammered on the table with his fist, shouting, "If you don't, then we will destroy you." Mr. Knöhr ordered party members to leave the club; instead, some of them resigned from the party.[2]

Werner had been pleased with the outcome. It seemed clear to him at the time that the Germans of San José, at least, were not going to be infected by the fever of nationalism that seemed to be gripping Germany.

Why, just this year, Karl Federspiel, a German bookstore owner and printer who had lived in Costa Rica since 1912, was elected president of the club precisely because he *was* antifascist! Karl had also decided to become a Costa Rican citizen after a few of the more outspoken local Nazi supporters threatened him with loss of his German citizenship. Most members felt that politics should be kept outside of the club, and Werner agreed.

But the notice Werner held in his hand was another reminder that he was German—and that Hitler and his policies could bring changes to the quiet, peaceful, apolitical life he lived with Starr. Werner did not want to be involved in any way. Yes, he'd had to register for military service at the German Counsel, but that seemed unimportant so far from Germany. But this ... this was here, at home.

He couldn't—wouldn't—vote. Starr was in total agreement. They decided to spend a week in the mountains during the time of the referendum. Others could vote if they wished, but Werner and Starr, with Sudi their cocker spaniel, spent the week of Easter at a small resort: swimming in the dammed-up river, reading mystery novels, eating, and being together. They had a wonderful time.

That December, Max Gurcke, Werner's father, came to visit, staying with them for about a month and then traveling to Guanacaste to visit Karl Oskar and his family. Max was very unlike his wife, Starr decided. To begin with, she felt comfortable calling him by his first name. In general, he was very quiet and reserved—although, after several beers, he could be very funny. And he never made comments about her housekeeping or what she should do about this or that. In fact, he seemed very much like Werni—which made him lovable too.

On occasion, what was happening in Germany came up in conversation. Max spoke positively of the changes Hitler was creating economically, but was less enthusiastic about Nazi attempts to expand Germany's borders. He was tired of war and feared Hitler's plans were too grandiose. Starr was genuinely sorry when they had to see him off for his return trip.

Top: Max Gurcke, Hermida
Kneeling: Pany and Karl Oskar

Life fell into a mostly pleasant pattern, though Starr felt Werner worked too hard. She knew he was almost obsessive about documenting every transaction, while his partner, Hans (pseudonym), was much more relaxed. She grudgingly admitted to herself that Hans was a help when he was there, but she thought he took too much time off. It seemed to her that he ought to shoulder more of the burden.

Werner's files were stuffed with papers dating back to his first days in Costa Rica, when he worked for a pharmaceutical company owned by C. W. Lohrengel, a distant relative. Werner began his own company in 1932, acting as a middleman between local retailers and foreign manufacturers of products like textiles, buttons, umbrellas, and watches. The paperwork multiplied as he spent more and more time at his desk. Now that his marriage was beyond the honeymoon stage, Werner was working again full tilt.

But Starr was able to pry Werni away from his ledgers for picnics, Sunday drives, movies, bowling, and swimming at the German Club. Neither of them was very fond of what seemed to be the main activity in San José, gossip-filled visiting at tea or coffee klatches.

On September 1, 1939, Starr and Werner awoke to air raid sirens around four thirty in the morning. That was really terrifying. They turned on the radio and learned that Hitler had invaded Poland. Werner and Starr spent the rest of the night talking. What next? Werner, worried about his family in Germany, was shaken by the possibility of another war. Neither he nor Starr could understand how *any* German would believe the stuff Hitler spouted, she explained in a letter to a friend. Shortly after that Britain declared war, and Werner's concern for his parents and youngest brother grew.

Tempering the apprehension Werner felt was his joy at Starr's pregnancy. They'd been trying for more than a year and had almost given up hope, so they were delighted. In December, armed with baby pamphlets and pages from a Montgomery Ward catalog sent by Liz, they ordered a crib and chest of drawers from Antonio Avila, one of the best local furniture makers.

Starr and Werner were very pleased with the results, which had been copied from pictures in the catalog. Painted with white enamel, the furniture was already installed in the nursery. Yes, the pieces had cost three hundred colones (about $60), but they were so well made and "just plain cute," that Starr was convinced they were worth it.

Life was easier for them now. They bought a locally made icebox and ordered a vacuum cleaner. Someday, they hoped to have a washing machine and a big stove. Electricity was available for a while each evening, and Starr and Werner planned to get a generator so that vacuuming could be done during the day.

Costa Rica was a secure, prospering country, and Werni's business was doing well so far. Though the young couple's contentment was clouded by concerns over his family in Germany, they were young, optimistic, and in love, looking forward to many happy years together.

"The Nazi Shadow" Endnotes

[1] For a full description of this odd episode, see Friedman, *Nazis and Good Neighbors*, 37–41. Around 275 people voted in Costa Rica, but most of those voters are not identified.

[2] January 29, 1944, Report on Hearing at Crystal City, Texas, DOJ Name Index File 146-13-2-1232, RG 60, NA; also Friedman, *Nazis and Good Neighbors*, 36–37. He describes the German Club, which had around two hundred members. Its activities were largely social, with a swimming pool, tennis courts, and the only bowling alley in San José. He also writes of the November 1934 failed attempt by Nazi sympathizers to take over the club, which must be the attempt Werner mentioned.

Babies and Blacklists

Starr walked into town on a cool winter day. She knew sixty degrees wasn't really cold by North American standards, but it certainly was here. She was to meet Werni, and they were going to shop for more baby supplies: diaper and sheet materials to be hemmed; blankets; rubber pads; and "various little shirts and night gowns … Little so-and-so will be born right in the hottest, most disagreeable part of the year, just before the rains start … I imagine just diapers and a mosquito net will keep 'it' happiest."

Werner and Starr always shopped together after her one attempt on her own. She had visited six stores before she got what she was looking for—three dozen safety pins and a dozen snaps! No one seemed to take her seriously, and they pretended not to understand when she tried to bargain for merchandise.

She needed him to properly intimidate the clerks with his much more flu-ent Spanish. Besides, he was a much better bargainer—and for larger items, that was important, especially now that they were trying to be very careful about money. After all, Germany had invaded Poland; it seemed that sooner or later, there'd be a wider conflict. Who knew what would happen to Werner's business then?

Werner walking to work
San José, Costa Rica

In February 1940, Starr wrote about "Snikkel fritz," as they called the baby, and the difficulties of gathering the proper baby supplies. For the first time, she decided to voice their concerns about the rise of Hitler.

We hear fairly regularly, but very much delayed, from Werner's family in Hamburg. They always write cheerfully and never mention hardships, but they're 100% Nazi, just completely fooled by all that nonsense they hear day in and day out. They just haven't the slightest idea of what's going on in the world around them except what the government wants to tell them. We thank Heaven we're here where our troubles are only financial—we'll at least always be able to express our opinions on the street and in letters.

My father told me about the day of my birth. He was almost beside himself when Starr told him she was having regular contractions. They were as ready as they could be; she had packed a suitcase, and he had been parking the car pointing toward town for the last month or so. He rushed her to the Clínica Bíblica in downtown San José, where she was taken away. Hours passed with no news. He was frantic. Baptized Lutheran, he had long ago given up going to church; but, afraid for Starr's life, he began to bargain with God. Werner was ready to do anything, *anything* if only Starr were all right.

Several hours later, while pacing in the lobby of the hospital, he saw his wife lying on a gurney, being taken to a regular hospital room. I had arrived. My mother—Werner's little Starrli—was wrapped in white sheets, her face so pale he was sure she was dead.

He was convinced she would survive only after he was allowed to talk to her. It had been a difficult delivery, but both she and I were fine. We went home together as a family ten days later.

A letter to Liz in July was full of news about me. After writing about diaper rash, formula, and all things baby, my mother decided to tell her friend a little about the uneasiness she and my father were having about their financial future.

> Lately we've been seriously reconsidering our old idea of buying a small farm and building us a small house. The idea was pure luxury at one time, a weekend house where we could spend summers. Now however it's getting to be an idea of economy and self-preservation. If we had our own land with a vegetable garden and maybe some chickens and a cow (!), we could at least live well for the duration of the war.... I can't imagine myself as a lady farmer or Werner as a gentleman one for that matter. But we could always learn.

In August, the British blacklist was published. My father and Karl Oskar were listed, as was my father's business. As companies became aware of the listings, orders began to dry up. My father also had other reasons for concern. He was increasingly uncomfortable with his business partner's behavior; Hans was mouthing Nazi propaganda more and more. He seemed to glory in the company of some of the most outspoken Nazi sympathizers in the area.

Too, local Nazis were attempting to take over the German Club once again. When some members started using Nazi salutes, my father decided—in consultation with my mother—to stop going to the club. After deliberating, he kept up his membership for business reasons. He also approached his business partner about disbanding their partnership, in part because of Hans's vocal support for Hitler and in part because business was much reduced.

In September 1940, my mother wrote again to Liz. She no longer tried to hide the worry that was beginning to dominate her life.

> We're being very cautious about our farming idea. If we only knew how long the war is going to last and how Werner's business will be after it, we might be able to make up our minds. As it is, we're very hesitant about spending so much money we might need if the war lasts for years and years more. Werner's parents in Germany are confident it will be over very soon, within a few weeks even, and that commerce will then simply bloom. I can't quite imagine that things will be very prosperous for a long time after such a war even provided it should end soon, which I hardly believe either.

As early as 1936, the president of the United States, Franklin Delano Roosevelt, became concerned about possible Nazi infiltration into Central and South America—and the danger this might pose for American security. By mid-1940, Federal Bureau of Investigation (FBI) agents were placed surreptitiously in each Latin-American country; in 1941, the Office of Strategical Services (OSS) ordered its Latin-American section to begin surveillance of all potential "enemy aliens" in the southern hemisphere. When my mother wrote Liz in May 1941— mostly about my antics and their excitement anticipating the birth of another baby in July—my parents' mail was being read, and their activities were being monitored.

My sister, Ingrid, was born on July 17, 1941—the same day that the U.S. president, in Proclamation 2497, declared some people to be on "The Proclaimed List of Certain Blocked Nationals." My father and Karl Oskar were on the list.

July 1941 - front: Werner, Heidi, Hermida
back: Starr, Karl Oskar, Pany

Realizing that this spelled the end of Werner's business, my parents decided to move out of San José to the more rural San Juan de Tibás, where they bought a tiny *finca* (farm). The finca—about an acre—had a little coffee plantation, squashes and bananas, and room for a big vegetable garden.

They even bought a cow, though that proved to be a mistake. Somehow, my father and the cow did not get along—he claimed they didn't understand each other—and it produced no milk, so eventually they sold it. The plan was to become self-sufficient by harvesting and selling coffee while growing as much of their own food as possible.

My father tenaciously continued to do what business he could. He drove off every morning, trying to find companies who would do business with him and attempting to collect moneys owed to him. He and his business partner dissolved the partnership, and in a carefully thought-out decision, he legally added my mother as his partner. They hoped that by doing so, they could ask companies to remit money owed to her as a U.S. citizen, instead of to him.

My mother stayed home with us babies; she had her hands full. The house, about four years old, had never been painted on the inside, and the floors were filthy with an accumulation of old wax and dust. My father helped, of course, but most of the housework and baby care fell on her shoulders, while he concentrated on the business, coffee plants, and garden.

the finca in San Juan de Tibás, Costa Rica, 1941

When the Costa Rican secretary of state gave notice that all resident aliens of German, Italian, or Japanese nationality were to register with his office at the beginning of the following year, my parents couldn't help but wonder why.

Trying to cajole my father out of the dark mood he was in over the loss of his business became increasingly difficult. Somehow he felt personally responsible and was often distraught, fearing he would be unable to provide for his young family. My mother just couldn't believe that things would get worse or didn't want to consider the possibility. She wrote to her brother and sister-in-law a few days before Christmas, trying to make sense of what was happening.

> You mustn't worry about us. At least up til now, no drastic measures have been taken against the Germans. The government is building a large camp for interning members of the enemy tribes but it has also assured us that our persons and property will be respected if we behave ourselves. Some property has been confiscated, like power plants and coffee benefices [probably *beneficios*, or plantations] belonging to Germans. Germans were arrested for a short while, and house searching is going on. We have already been very thoroughly and rather humiliatingly searched but, we believe, pronounced innocent of firearms, dinamite [sic] and propaganda leaflets. We don't believe the blacklist will be considered as a reason for internment since half Costa Rica is on it. Of course, I'm still a little anxious about that enormous camp under construction but anyway we're going to celebrate Christmas together.
>
> I have thought a bit about going to the States but only if Werner were sent out of the country and we couldn't go with him. But even then I

have the farm and car and kids and dog and how could I manage all that? On the whole tho, we're ever so much more cheerful than we were a week or so ago. Costa Rica's participation in the Situation is mostly treated jokingly here—after all, we have no army, no navy, no airplanes, just a few policemen and some not too bright detectives. One restriction that has been placed on Germans (and Italians and Japanese) is that they must secure a special permit to travel from one canton [district] to another. We are fortunately in the San José district so we can go to town when we please.

In another letter, she mentioned the difficulty of getting a travel permit. In order to visit friends in a different canton, my parents had to get up early; rouse, dress, and feed us girls; then go into town to the police station for the permit. There they waited and waited some more, money in hand, for the required *mordida*—or bribe. At the other end of the trip, they had to take the permit to that canton's police department. By the time they actually got to friends, Ingrid and I were cranky and tired, and it was almost time to head back to home.

But she could handle it, she wrote; she could handle anything as long as Werner was with her. Please God, she wrote, keep him with her.

"It Is a War to the Death"

On his thirty-third birthday, January 10, 1942, my father sent a letter to the Costa Rican secretary of state as required, registering his name and address as a resident alien. My parents spent hours thinking about how to make it clear that Werner was not a danger to the country, in spite of his place of birth. He wrote in Spanish.

> As a German subject, I want to make it known that I have been in this country for twelve years, dedicating myself to business. I married a North American woman and my life has been spent on work and home. I belong to no party nor do I support Nazi ideas. I want to say this for future record. I'd also like to say that my two little daughters are registered with the North American Consulate.

Neither of them was aware that Werner was now labeled "one of the most dangerous German nationals in the country" in a secret FBI memo. The memo, sent to the Alien Enemy Control unit in Washington D.C., stated,

> During 1941, several reports were received from a source generally reliable to the effect that Gurcke was a German merchant in Costa Rica who possessed Nazi sympathies and was considered to be one of the most dangerous German nationals in the country. It was reported that he and his wife were voting members of the German Club of San Jose [sic].[1]

He spent less time in town now. What work he could do there took only a few hours. He picked the coffee harvest—hot, dirty, physical labor—and he and my mother spread it out to dry. Since they had no equipment for roasting it, they sold the crop to a larger concern. He also planted a variety of vegetables, many of them succumbing almost immediately to insects and animal predators. Doggedly, he replanted.

There were mango, peach, papaya, loquat, banana, plantain, lemon, and orange trees on their land, all doing fairly well. And my mother was heartened by some roses and chrysanthemums in bloom. Just before the rainy season, she hoped they could plant a lawn around the house, along with more flowers. The water they had available in the dry season they saved for the vegetables.

She wrote to Liz in February, detailing the attempts she and my father were making to get house, garden, and life in order. Her letter was also read by a U.S. censor, who reported passages he or she felt pertinent, commenting in the report, "The greater part of this letter, dealing with a mother's household routine, reflects an intelligent and sane mi[n]d, a joyful and equinamical [sic] spirit, and an honest and sincere character."[2] (Passages the censor quoted as politically pertinent are in italics.)

Right now [Werner is] *the chief cause of all my worry. He's still with me, thank God, but I can't help wondering for how long. A short time ago, 38 Germans, supposedly those belonging to the Nazi party here, were deported very quietly and suddenly. Goodness knows Werner never had anything to do with the Nazis and we hardly came in contact with the German colony as a whole. We had our few friends and minded our own business always. But since Werner's firm got on the blacklist for no reason that we know of, there could easily be another injustice of the same nature. A large concentration camp is being built here too; for whom is the big question. We've done all we can think of to help—gone to the American consul—I'm still an American, and have written to the Government, stating our innocence of any conspiring against it. Werner has to have a special permit to travel, that is, to go from here to town or to friends out of town, etc. Now there's talk about our having to give up our radio and camera, which would be a shame but which we'd gladly do if that were all that would happen to us.*

Werner's business has, of course, been completely ruined. He's still winding up the last few affairs but spends most of his time at home now, working here and helping me tend the babies. If we could only be sure he could stay safely with us and if people weren't dying by the thousands all over the world, we could be pretty happy on our enforced vacation. By living economically and raising our own vegetables and having a cow and chickens (possibly), we will be able to weather this time financially (I think, and if it doesn't last too long.) … Werner, of course, doesn't hear from his family in Germany any more. They must be sick from worry about us, especially as the German newspapers are probably full of propaganda about the persecution of Germans here. We tried to send them a telegram but it's not permitted.… Such a lot has happened to all of us and it has happened so fast that we haven't time to sit and brood long over one particular event. Private events and world events are all so closely tied up together these days but I find I can still delight in my newly made curtains in the kitchen and never give Pearl

Harbor or Singapore a thought while I'm trying to dodge Ingrid's hands and feet and land the … spoonful of Pablum in her ever moving mouth and not in her eye or mine. Which is certainly some kind of a comment on my nature or maybe on human nature in general…. What would I do if Werner were to be shipped off to God knows where for some undetermined time? I'm sure I don't know how I'd manage. Meanwhile I feed babies and make curtains and am content.

In April Lt. Col. Andino sent further information from the American Legation in San José to military intelligence offices in Washington D.C. He reported that Starr Pait Bruce was receiving mail from firms in South America and the United States on business matters, and that she was Werner's wife. This was treated as "alleged German subversive activities in America," and a file was opened on her.[3] Their scheme to circumvent the blacklist had failed.

My father was profoundly troubled when he came home from town on June 28. Local newspapers, including the *La Tribuna* he held in his hand, had a full page of the names of people and companies on the Lista Negra o Proclamada Para Costa Rica (Costa Rican Black or Proclaimed List). The vicious banner above the names declared: "Do not buy from the enemies of the democracy. The money you give will be used to attack you. Eliminate economic dealings with the sympathizers of Gestapo crimes. It is a war to the death: You are totally against them or with them…." It was signed "La Directiva de la Acción Democrática Costarricense" (Board of Directors, Costa Rican Democratic Action Committee). Werner hadn't realized until the moment he read those words how widespread the demonization of Axis nationals had become. He was also shaken when he saw that my mother's name had been added to the list.

Then, a few days later, the Costa Rican military raided our home, confiscating my parents' old hunting rifle, camera and radio. It was the loss of the camera that hurt the most; there would be no more pictures of Ingrid or me.

My parents tried to carry on as usual. There was nothing else they could do, and both house and garden needed enormous amounts of work. They labored each day until nearly exhausted. We, their daughters, were the only bright spot. They lavished us with attention and love.

By this time, the government had established an agency, the Junta de Custodia de la Propiedad Enemiga (Enemy Property Custodial Board), which took custody of the property of all blacklisted persons and businesses in the country. The original purpose of the agency was to keep German assets from being used to finance Nazi activity. Those blacklisted could apply to receive monthly amounts of their own funds, but only after forms were filed and government levies paid. Applying was both time-consuming and humiliating, and the only way to speed the process was to add a hefty bribe for the official in charge.

Starr with Ingrid and Heidi
our last picture from Costa Rica, early 1942

July brought more bad news. A German submarine torpedoed a ship in Limón, killing twenty-four crewmen. That led to protests and a riot in San José, injuring seventy-six and damaging one hundred and twenty-three buildings. One hundred Germans were immediately imprisoned, and the rest were confined to house arrest.[4] Karl Oskar was jailed on July 4, while my father was placed under house arrest.

It fell on my mother now to drive into town, trying to collect money that was still owed to the business. And people paid. They were very nice about it, to her relief. She also had to tackle the Junta de Custodia to gain access to our family's savings.

My father was chagrined to be so powerless. After over a week of staying in the house and garden, he was wild with restlessness. He decided to take a walk at dusk, unable to contain himself. My mother insisted on going with him. We children were left in the care of María Rodríguez, a neighbor. Whether someone saw him away from the finca and reported it, they never found out, but several days later—on the fifteenth—he was arrested and taken to a prison in San José.

What had happened? Was he asked to report to the police station, or was he picked up by Costa Rican police in a late-night raid of our home? Other families in Latin America reported their men simply disappeared, snatched off the streets. Some were gone for months before they were able to write their loved ones from a camp in the United States or from Germany or Japan. My mother only told me of the walk she took with my father the last time they were free together in Costa Rica. I didn't think to press for more details.

July 17, [1942]

Dear Charles and Virginia,

Since day before yesterday Werner has been in the local Penitenciary [sic]. For a week before he had had house arrest and we were happy. We haven't the remotest idea why they arrested him or what's going to happen to him and the many others there. And they won't let me see anyone to find out the charges against him or to do any explaining. Heidi wakes up at nite screaming, "Papi, Papi" and today is Ingrid's first birthday.

Thank God, the kids are well, and I have a wonderful older woman to help me and leave them with when I drive to San José to spend a short 15 minutes with Werner and do all the chores.

As you see, my heart is breaking—

with all my love, Starr

About a week later, my father, uncle, and the other prisoners were moved to the newly constructed prison my mother had mentioned in an earlier letter to her brother and sister-in-law—called a concentration camp by both Costa Rican and United States officials. When my mother heard that the men were sleeping on the cold, hard floor, she was furious. Somehow, she wrestled a mattress into their little Opel and drove it to the prison. Her Werni would have a bed!

She was able to visit for about fifteen minutes two or three times a week, bringing food and flowers. Men and women had to stand apart in the central courtyard during these visits, and armed guards were stationed both in the area and above, in watchtowers. Germans were the sole prisoners there, as far as she could tell.

Historian Max Friedman paints a grim picture of these prisons. The first was filled to overflowing, necessitating the construction of the new concentration camp to house more inmates. The prisoners themselves threw out filthy, vermin-infested bedding, voluntarily whitewashed the building, and sprayed cells with insecticide. Families brought in food whenever possible, since meals were of poor quality and insufficient quantity. Special services at the prison, like private rooms for conjugal visits or better food, could be had by bribing the guards. German prisoners were interrogated in the office of the director of the secret police; they were offered more lenient treatment in exchange for cash or sex. No one was released from the prison without U.S. assent.[5]

Did my father or uncle pay for special treatment? Were the wives of prisoners also offered leniency for their husbands in exchange for sex? Was my mother approached? My aunt? I don't know. My mother never mentioned any details beyond the mattress incident and the brief visits she was allowed.

I have a sketch of the prison, done by my father from memory about a year after his imprisonment. The central area is vast and empty. The high walls—topped with tall wire barricades—dwarf two tiny benches, while a distant figure in the guard tower holds a gun. There is only one small human touch, a sign reading "Cantina" on a wall.

María, our neighbor, stepped in to help my mother on a daily basis. Quiet, calm, and sweet, she quickly won the hearts of both of us children. Her help allowed Mom to devote her time to everything else that needed attention: the house, garden, food shopping, and collecting of debts owed. Local rum helped her get through the evenings and put her to sleep, she told Charles and Virginia in an August 1 letter.

> I am managing somehow—financially I'm all right, if the War doesn't last an eternity ... In the two weeks that I've been alone, I've become a little more accustomed to my fate and recovered from the first black mood of despair.
>
> All of our neighbors ... have been terribly nice—everyone would help me if they only could. Which makes the thought of ever having to leave Costa Rica forcibly extremely distasteful. During these last two weeks, I've come to the conclusion that the Costa Ricans are just about the kindest people on earth, a conclusion that gives me the basis of a hope that they can't possibly detain Werner for very long.... don't worry about me—I'm in the friendliest possible country; what has happened to us was inevitable, the times being what they are.

And on August 2,

> I don't know what Werner's plans are for the future; I only hope they include staying here. One possibility: that of being shipped to Germany, makes me shudder with horror, and Werner agrees with me that it's about the worst thing that could happen to us. My last letter to you (since Werner's arrest) was ... returned to me for reasons which now seem to me obvious and adequate, hence my delay in replying and hence the formality of this letter. *Please* don't worry about me. I *think* I can manage, at least I did today and I'm sure I can tomorrow.

Though he was imprisoned, my father was not idle. On September 8, he wrote in English to the U.S. legation, requesting that he be allowed to return to

San Juan de Tibás—under house arrest if need be—so that he could help and protect his family. Concerned that his wife would become ill from exhaustion, he was also deeply distressed by his internment and the reasons behind it.

> In a last effort to solve the situation of my family, I, Werner Gurcke, now interned in the Concentration Camp in San José, Costa Rica, sincerely ask to consider the following points:
>
> 1) My wife, Starr Pait Bruce, an American citizen, now living in San Juan de Tibás with our two girls, Heidi (30 months) and Ingrid (14 months), both registered at the American Consulate, San José, has no family protection at all because her only brother, Charles Pait Jr. is living in the States at Los Angeles, California, my brother is interned here with me and my parents are living in Hamburg, Germany. Her parents are dead.
>
> 2) There does not exist a real motive for my internment otherwise than that I am a German, because never in my life I had something to do with politics, propaganda or else, even so my name and that of my wife are included in the Proclaimed list. But this yourselves know best. Even if you do think otherwise, there must be a mistake and I am sure to convince you to it, if you will have the kindness to present to me the reasons you had to include our names in the above mentioned list, or to tell me the facts why the Costa Rican Government did have the necessity to intern me in this camp.
>
> 3) It is quite easy to understand that in case of any prolongation of my internment, my wife will suffer the most, being overworked with the care of the two babies and the household and beyond the reach of any kind of family protection. As it is, I do fear that in a short time, this state will undermine her health in every aspect, and therefore do appeal to you for help, i.e. to do your utmost to obtain from the Costa Rican Government the permission for me to live again, even under arrest, in my wife's little farm in San Juan de Tibás, Calle Llorente.

He wrote even more emotionally on September 29.

> When I wrote you the last time I did it because I thought that the fate of three American citizens i.e. my wife and her two children cannot be indifferent to you. I still have the same opinion.
>
> It is therefore my duty to recall to your mind that the prolongation of my internment will inevitable lead to disaster, i.e. not in our domestic happiness or at the moment with regard to funds, but in the way of overexertion beyond my wife's strengths.

Please remember that from the day of our marriage (January 17th, 1936 in Santa Cruz, California) my sole effort has been to safeguard the health and well-being of my family.

Under the present circumstances I find myself, this is not possible and as I cannot believe that the continuance of such a state of great danger to my family does agree upon your conscientiousness as legal representative of the United States Government, sincerely ask to do something about it, before it is too late.

There was no response to either letter.

My mother tried everything she could think of to get him out. She went to the American Counsel and was told *they* had nothing to do with it—it was the Costa Ricans. So she went to the Costa Ricans and was told, "Oh, it's the Americans." *They* had nothing to do with it. She soon realized the counsels were working together, and she would get no help from either group. Neither of my parents realized the depth of United States' involvement in my father's detention and our subsequent deportation.

While my parents struggled to free themselves from their quagmire, Charles, my mother's brother, became peripherally involved. He had been acting as his sister's agent in the settling of their mother's estate. There were a number of parcels of land in their inheritance, and when Charles sold one, he would send her share of the proceeds. Sometime that summer, the censor returned a letter he had sent Starr, with a note indicating Charles needed a special license to do any sort of business with her.

The full title of the license required was the jawbreaking "License to Engage in a Foreign Exchange Transaction, Transfer of Credit, Payment, Export or Withdrawal from the United States, or the Earmarking, of Gold or Silver Coin or Bullion or Currency, or the Transfer, Withdrawal or Exportation of, or Dealing in, Evidences of Indebtedness or Evidences of Ownership of Property." Once Charles filled out the application and returned it, he received a letter from the Federal Reserve Bank of San Francisco asking him to explain why he needed a license—to which he replied on August 8 that he didn't know; the censor had demanded it. By 1943, the red tape must have been resolved, because my father notes checks from Charles to Starr in his financial records. But that was of no help in 1942.

Rumors were rampant about what was going to happen to the prisoners. An earlier group of imprisoned men had been deported very quietly, but no one knew where they had been taken. All my parents could do was wait and worry.

At the beginning of December, just as my mother tucked Ingrid and me into bed, two Costa Rican policemen came to the door of our home in Tibás to arrest her. She was given only time enough to collect her two sleepy daughters and gather up her purse and a sweater. We were taken to the German Club, which had been turned into a holding facility for the wives and children of the men in the concentration camp.

There were no preparations for us, as my mother remembered it. She was able to hire a horse and cart to have a baby crib delivered the next day, but she and most of the women slept, as best they were able, on the floor that first night, taking what comfort they could in having their children beside them.

German Club, San José, Costa Rica, 1930's

Rumors spread that we were going to be deported, but the women were never told anything officially. No one knew whether their husbands would be traveling with them. The bathroom facilities were abysmally inadequate, so dirty diapers were washed out in the swimming pool. Food was sufficient, but not geared to the children. "It was a nightmare," my mother told me years later. The women were kept at the club for about a week and then sent home because, according to the grapevine, the ship hadn't arrived.

Weary and infuriated, my mother was determined to find out what was going to happen to us. She decided to tackle the staff of the Costa Rican Seguridad Pública—the police force. After approaching several people, she found a sympathetic official, Jorge Hernández, who told her that our whole family was on a list of aliens to be deported. This list had been drawn up by the U.S. legation. He may also have told her that we were being sent to the United States.

(For some time, the U.S. legation had been turning away Axis citizens who wanted visas. They insisted the Costa Rican government not accept applicants who wished to become citizens and demanded slower procedures for those who'd already filed. The pressure on Costa Rican officials was to be applied in a subtle, secretive way that could not be traced to the United States. When a *written* memo was sent by the U.S. Embassy to the Costa Rican Foreign Office some time later, listing more people approved by Alien Enemy Control officials in the United States for deportation and internment, J.M. Cabot, chief of the Central America Division, wrote to officials ... "we should rap the Embassy sharply over the knuckles for such an indiscreet act."[6])

My mother immediately applied for a new passport. Her application was approved with the proviso that the passport was valid only for immediate return to the United States and was of limited duration—until January 17, 1943.

Around December 22, much to everyone's surprise, the German men, all those "dangerous" alien enemies, were furloughed from prison to spend Christmas with their families. Ingrid and I greeted our father with suspicion. He had become a stranger in the five months he'd been gone.

My parents spent much of their precious time together trying to decide on what to pack and what to leave. They were allowed to take only what they could carry. They wandered from room to room, weighing the affection each had for the material things of their lives, knowing they might never again see what they left behind.

María, our neighbor, offered to care for Sudi our cocker spaniel, and my parents gave her money to have a large wooden trunk made, in which she would store our photograph albums and books, as well as other valued possessions. These included wood sculptures and artists' drawings my parents had gathered on trips around the countryside; crocheted doilies and linens hand-embroidered by Frieda, my German grandmother; and family letters. María promised to send the trunk to us when it was possible to do so.

The unusual plants Starr and Werner had collected during their trips into the mountains would have to be abandoned. The beautiful little baby crib, the wonderful new icebox, the carefully sewn curtains—all left behind. They contacted Costa Rican friends who were willing to help sell their car and home and keep the money safe if they could.

On New Year's Eve, my parents stole rare quiet time together. Knowing they would soon be leaving Costa Rica and fearing that my father might be sent forcibly to Germany—perhaps alone—they didn't talk about the future.

Instead, my father reminisced, telling my mother more about his early experiences in Costa Rica, before the country became so civilized and modern. She thought, but did not say, *Civilized? Modern?* He showed her page after page of photographs.

There was his first, shared room in a San José boarding house; here, his office, where he both lived and worked when he began his business. As Werner turned the pages of the album, his life in Costa Rica unfolded: he smiles broadly, striding down the street in a suit and hat; he and his friends grin wickedly at the camera while swimming nude at Tres Ríos; he and an old flame stand in front of the beautiful little church in Orosi; a swarm of young men and women surround someone's new car. Here he and Karl Oskar pose at the summits of the Irazú and Poas volcanos, looking with awe at the burbling, smoking craters; there he lounges on a sailboat for the first time, master of the sea. There are many, many pictures of laughing friends, arm in arm, delighted to be in Costa Rica together. There are jungle birds and monkeys, placid brown rivers and rushing mountain rivulets, brightly painted carretas (horse- or oxen-drawn carts with gaudy designs painted on the wheels), and the colorful small towns of the countryside.

Spreading out the map he bought over ten years before, when he first arrived, Werner carefully showed her where each picture had been taken. How he loved the bustle and lively confusion of San José! The food, the pace of life, even the sound of Spanish seemed like home. The sense of liberation Werner felt upon leaving Germany was more than simply that of a son leaving his parents for the first time. In Costa Rica, he told Starr, he had felt that all things were possible for him and had set out to prove it.

Now war had followed him here, tearing apart the life he'd built, and he could not even protect his wife and small children. He felt deeply burdened by feelings of inadequacy and obligation, just as he had as a child in the first war. Werner and Starr sat quietly, holding hands. They were numbed, unable to absorb the enormity of their loss. There was nothing more that they could do. Life was out of their control.

During the night, a thief entered the house through our unlocked bedroom window. The next morning, they found a number of things missing, including my mother's purse. The purse, of brown alligator, contained money, her driver's license and birth certificate, $100 in traveler's checks of $10 each, her passport, and three keys to the baggage she was taking with her on the ship. They reported the theft to the police that day, and my mother went to the vice consul at the U.S. Legation, Livingston D. Watrous, to request a new passport. He wrote out a report but did not issue her new papers.

"It Is a War to the Death" Endnotes

[1] Federal Bureau of Investigation (FBI) memo, undated. Department of Justice stamp marked October 30, 1943, Alien Enemy Unit, DOJ Name Index File 146-13-2-1232, RG 60, NA. (In Max Paul Friedman's *Nazis and Good Neighbors*, 112, he mentions that D. G. Tenney, who conducted a postwar review of Costa Rican key documents and recommendations, called U.S. military attaché Lt. Col. E. Andino—the probable source of the reports on my father—"one of the most unreliable intelligence officers in the employ of the United States Government.")

[2] United States of America National Censorship Report, 21 February 1942, 740.00112A, Central Decimal Files, NA.

[3] Lt. Col. E. Andino, Office of the Military Attaché, San José, Costa Rica, undated. Recorded 10 April 1942 by DOJ, Central Decimal Files, NA. (In Latin America, the mother's maiden name is appended last. Starr's mother's maiden name was Bertha Bruce; therefore, Starr would have been known as Starr Pait Bruce until she married, when "de Gurcke" would be added to her name. Werner also used Werner Gurcke Hickfang, his mother's maiden name, on occasion.)

[4] Friedman, *Nazis and Good Neighbors*, 171–72.

[5] Friedman, *Nazis and Good Neighbors*, 149.

[6] J. M. Cabot to Wright and Bonsal, 15 November 1943, in "Important Papers," Name Files of Enemy Aliens 1942–48, Box 31, SWP, RG 59, NA. The words legation and embassy seem to be used interchangeably in these documents. A legation was an office of lower diplomatic standing than an embassy.

COSTA RICAN PHOTOGRAPHS, 1929–35

1929 Werner, left-Karl Oskar, right

1929 trip to San Isidro—Werner far left

the ranch near Tilaran from right: Werner, unidentified man, Hermida, Pany, Karl Oskar, two unidentified men

Karl Oskar, left; Werner, right probably Arenal volcano in background, Guanacaste, undated

Werner, left-Karl Oskar, right
Poas or Irazú volcano,
undated

1932 sailing trip, Werner, right

DEPORTATION

On January 2, my father and the other men reported back to prison. Around the country, wives and mothers finished preparations for deportation. My mother stayed on at the finca doing final packing. In mid-January 1943, the women and children were again rounded up and taken back to the German Club, where we waited for another week "under indescribable sanitary conditions," as my mother wrote later to Liz. No attempts had been made to clean since our last stay. The pool, last used to rinse out diapers, was now a reeking, fermenting sewer. Many of the children, including Ingrid and me, had "pink eye"—conjunctivitis. Others began coughing and developed runny noses.

Around January 20, the women were told to get ready to leave. We were taken by bus to the railroad station, where we met the men. Since families were allowed to sit together, Karl Oskar, Pany, and Hermida joined us. My parents were grateful to have extra hands to help get us wriggling, restless girls and their luggage onto the train.

The trip took all night, purposely, so that as few people as possible would see us in transit. When we arrived in Puntarenas, the Pacific port, the children were given canned milk straight out of the cans—the first nourishment provided since the trip had begun. Many children, already queasy from the trip, vomited it up immediately.

A launch came and picked us up in groups, taking us out to a ship anchored some distance from shore. There, all luggage was checked over and, except for immediate essentials, stored. We were given receipts, signed by a captain of the U.S. military police—Leonard C. Kincaid—who also confiscated all the money we had been allowed to take out of Costa Rica ($50 U.S. dollars for each adult). Valid passports and visas were seized, although my mother was allowed to keep her old, canceled one.

The ship was the U.S. Army transport (USAT) *Puebla*. The men were separated from their families and housed down in the hold. My mother, Ingrid, and I were assigned cabin space with two other women and their two little girls. For over a week, the ship stayed in port with blackout restrictions in place. For over a week, until the ship sailed, no one was allowed on deck. No portholes could be opened. It was hot and humid, and the air filled with the stink of dirty diapers and old sweat.

The other women had taken over the corner of the L-shaped cabin that had bunks built into it. There was no other furniture, so soldiers brought in a bunk bed—a ramshackle, old metal thing, with upper and lower berths but no railings. Fearing her babies would fall out, Mom asked the soldiers to take it away, leaving only stained and shabby mattresses.

As she tried to settle in, she suddenly realized that she had forgotten her old purse at home. The most immediate need was a comb. Leaving us in the care of her cabin-mates, she wandered around the ship, hoping to find someplace she could buy one. When she met a sailor, she explained her quest. He shook his head but, seeing her eyes fill with tears, he took his own comb out of his pocket and gave it to her. His kindness, after all the past difficult months, overwhelmed her, and she retreated to the cabin, crying. (Over fifty years later, when she told me this story, her tears still spilled freely.)

Four months later, María Rodríguez, our former neighbor in Costa Rica, was finally given permission to send the "pocketbook" my mother had left behind, with "1 box of powder, 1 nailfile not more that 4 1/2 inches long, 2 spoons, 1 change purse, 1 lipstick, 1 handkerchief, 1 pencil, hairpins and safety pins, and 1 comb."[1]

Many of the children, including Ingrid and me, were sick now with infections picked up in the confines of the dirty, overcrowded German Club where we were held prior to deportation. Feverish and fussy, we were difficult to comfort in the cramped space of the cabin. Diapers had to be washed by hand, then hung around the cabin to dry. Because it was so hot and my sister and I had rashes already, Mom decided not to diaper us at night.

During the day, she piled the mattresses, damp with her daughters' urine, in a corner, so that we could move around the cabin. The whole experience seemed very, very makeshift; it was rumored that authorities hadn't expected women and children, only men prisoners. There was also a rumor that the *Puebla* was a hospital ship coming from the Far East someplace and that there were wounded soldiers aboard. "Rumors," she told me years later, "were flying all over the place."

Initially, the women and children were allowed barely twenty minutes to eat. Bedraggled and hot, the families emerged from below—only to see the American crew, dressed in clean, pressed clothes, seated at other tables. That first meal my mother ate nothing, while she tried to hurry me when I dawdled, and tempt Ingrid, who was too excited to be fed willingly. The only thing that made that meal bearable was that my father was there, waiting tables along with a few other men.

The men had volunteered in hopes of seeing their families and also, perhaps, of getting more to eat. The prisoners in the hold were only fed twice a day. Ingrid and I, along with the children of the other "waiters," clamored for attention, but the prisoners were not allowed to speak with their wives or children. The scene was bedlam.

At future meals, the women got around that ban by talking to their husbands in Spanish or German while pretending to speak to each other. Since the guards seemed to know neither language, lopsided communication could take place. Problems with feeding small children were resolved when authorities allowed the teenaged girls to stay below with the children while the mothers ate. The mothers then brought food down for all the youngsters.

The ship left Puntarenas on January 26. There were no ports of call until it reached San Pedro, California. Daily inspections were held. Though the cramped cabins were overcrowded with women and children, a sailor decided that the women in our cabin could not go on deck one day, because they'd hung washed diapers around the room to dry. Voice shaking with rage when she told me this story half a century later, my mother asked, "Where *were* we expected to hang diapers?"

What was it like for my father and the other men down in the bowels of the ship? I imagine the heat and the stench of unwashed men, vomit, and open-bucket latrines. Did they have any bedding? Was there adequate water for drinking, if not for bathing? Were they ever allowed a breath of fresh air? My father never talked about his experience, even to my mother. When she asked, he simply turned away.[2]

By the time the ship docked at the immigration detention station on Terminal Island, San Pedro, California, at 7:00 AM on February 6, many more children were fevered and coughing. The faces, hands, and arms of many children and some adults had blistering sores, crusted with thick, yellow exudate. Both Ingrid and I were very sick, but Ingi was the sickest. Our mother was also coughing.

The women and children were led to a dorm-like room with beds and clean sheets and a big bathroom. Of course, there were bars across the windows, but after the ship voyage the new setting seemed like pure luxury. The men were taken away; where, no one knew.

"Deportation" Endnotes

[1] Report by American Diplomatic and Consular Officer, San José, Costa Rica, 21 May 1943, 740.00112A, Special War Problems Division, N.A.

[2] Harvey C. Gardiner, *Pawns in a Triangle of Hate: The Peruvian Japanese and the United States* (Seattle: University of Washington Press, 1981) mentions that 168 Japanese and 5 Germans were deported from Peru in January 1943 and taken to Panama, where they were joined by fifteen other Peruvian Japanese. They then boarded the USAT *Puebla*, which picked up our group in Costa Rica before sailing to San Pedro, California, where we arrived on February 6, 1943. Gardiner states that the Peruvian prisoners were expected to do chores, which included washing the American guards' clothing. Perhaps all the Costa Rican men were also assigned work.

IMMIGRATION DETENTION STATION, TERMINAL ISLAND (SAN PEDRO, CALIFORNIA)

Prior to our family's arrival in California, authorities grappled with the fact that my mother appeared to be a U.S. citizen yet was alleged to have engaged in subversive activities. Her status was addressed in a note from the Department of Justice Alien Enemy Control Unit:

> January 16, 1943
>
> Memo for Mr. Burling
> Re: Star [sic] Paite [sic] Bruce Gurcke, wife of Werner Gurcke
>   At 3:40 Mr. Nicholas telephoned that she is coming up from Costa Rica: that she is a 'sort of American citizen'; that State does not wish her released immediately, but sent to concentration camp with her husband, and so held until FBI, which is interested, has a chance to question and investigate.[1]

In order to legalize our deportation and imprisonment, the U.S. government issued arrest warrants that were served on my parents as soon as we arrived. On February 6, "under the authority of the agreement between the United States and the Republic of Costa Rica," warrants were issued by Francis Biddle, attorney general, approving my parents' detention until further notice as "person[s] whom I deem dangerous to the public peace and safety of the United Nations."[2]

The day after we arrived at the detention station, my parents were given a hearing by an immigration and naturalization board of special inquiry composed of three members. The hearing had one point only: "These proceedings are for the purpose of determining your *right* to enter the United States," according to the official board record (italics added). The instructions went on, "[You have the right to have a friend or relative present] ... provided ... that the friend or relative is not and will not be employed by you as counsel or attorney ... [and] is not an agent ... of an immigrant aid or other similar society or organization."

Members of the board asked about past travel, country of nationality, and occupation. When my father was questioned about future plans, he told them he

45

would like to remain in the United States if possible. Since their life in Costa Rica was completely disrupted, he and my mother apparently had decided to try to get to the California beach house when, and if, they were freed. After that, who knew?

The hearing was adjourned at 6:30 PM and resumed the next morning. At that time, my mother, sister, and I were admitted as citizens, but my father was denied admission to the United States on the grounds that he did not have the proper papers—no passport, visa, or "bordercrossing identification card"—and that "he is an immigrant not in possession of a valid immigration visa as required by the Immigration Act of 1924 and not exempted from the presentation thereof by said Act or regulations made thereunder." (Remember, valid passports and visas were confiscated by authorities when the prisoners boarded the *Puebla* in Puntarenas.)

Chairman A. B. Coon then told him, "You are further informed that after your deportation as an excluded alien you may not reapply for admission to the United States within one year from the date of your deportation, unless … you have applied to the Attorney General for permission to reapply for admission and he has granted your request." The report concluded, "Alien to be detained at: Crystal City, Texas."3

When my mother was asked whether she and the children wanted to be released or be permitted to accompany her husband, she chose to keep the family together. Our family had been separated too long already, and she and my father were concerned that if he were left alone, he would end up someplace like Bismarck, North Dakota, the location of a detention facility for single prisoners at Fort Lincoln. They were both afraid he would eventually be sent back to Germany. Whether my mother really would have been released is questionable, given the January 16 Alien Control Unit memo expressing FBI interest in her and the warrant for her arrest issued February 6.

Jerre Mangione wrote in *An Ethnic at Large* (321–22),

> For me, one of the most curious aspects of the internment program was the presence in the camps of several thousand men and women (with their children) from Latin-American countries who, at the request of our State Department, had been seized by their own governments as potentially dangerous alien enemies and handed over to American authorities. Compounding the bizarreness of the program was the Machiavellian device that was contrived to legalize their detention by the Immigration Service. This consisted of escorting the Latin-Americans over our borders, then charging them with "illegal entry" into the country. As an Immigration Service camp commander told me, "Only in wartime could we get away with such fancy skullduggery."

On February 9, INS officials called my mother in for a lengthy interrogation. There were only two men there: Theron F. Culp, who identified himself as acting immigration inspector and special inspector, and Walter F. Reiss, clerk and stenographer. Starr was somewhat flattered when one asked the other, "Who's the girl? Why is the girl here?" to the matron who brought her to the room. She thought that was complimentary, because she was around thirty and felt anything but girlish after her recent experiences.

Over and over, Culp asked her to describe Werner's business and to name the firms with which he dealt. When had she gone to Germany? Why? Who were her associates while she had studied in Munich? How had she met Werner? How many Germans lived in Costa Rica in December 1942? How many lived in San José? He asked her for the names of all their social contacts and the names of all Werner's relatives.

What did each firm Werner represented manufacture? When she responded— watches from the Hamilton Watch Company in the United States; umbrellas from another U.S. firm; soaps and baby articles by one house in Germany; wool, yarns, dresses, sweaters, and hosiery from another; embroidered goods from a firm in Madeira; textiles by a Japanese factory—the questioner didn't seem to believe her. He was particularly suspicious of Werner's importation of wool to Central America, a subject he returned to several times, even after she patiently explained that San José is on a high plateau and can be quite cool.

She was asked why Werner had been deported. The only reason she gave was that he was German. "He has never done or been in any way connected with the Nazi Party. He has never been with the military in Germany. We hardly know the Nazis, dislike the Nazis thoroughly and always have. His brother, so help me, is friendly to the Nazi theories, his older brother who is here with us, and his mother and father are too ... but he is not and I definitely mean that. And we loved Costa Rica."

She answered these questions as carefully and calmly as she could, but sparks flew when the interrogator asked again, "Isn't it a fact that your husband belongs to the Nazi Party?"

A — No! A thousand times no! He never had anything to do with it.

Q — Why did he have different ideas than the other members of his family along those lines?
A — I don't know. Probably because he is smarter. Maybe because he is married to me....

Q—What form of government does he believe in?
A —Ours.

Q—Has he ever resided in the United States?
A —No, but residing in Costa Rica is like this. Costa Rica is a republic and a good one. You live there free and happily.... If you knew, it would be so obvious he can't be in sympathy with the Nazis because his very existence from when he was very young has been here ... He worked so hard and made good money ... enough to take a trip to Germany and take a trip to marry me and raise a family and all, and in what other country could you do anything like that except Costa Rica and the United States....

The interrogation went on.

Q—How long was your husband in a concentration camp in Costa Rica?
A —Six months.

Q—Why was he in the concentration camp?
A —I don't know.

Q—What charges were placed against him?
A —I don't know any definite charges. I only know rumors. One was that people passed our house and heard strange noises at night.

Q—What strange noise was heard?
A —... They might have heard ... our electric refrigerator, which worked only at night ... and also the vacuum cleaner, which I could only use at night too because of the current only at night. Another rumor was that we had meetings of German people at our house—of many, many German people.

She refuted that rumor to the interrogator and said these were the only "ridiculous charges" she and Werner ever heard against them.[4]

My mother's memories of interrogation varied markedly from the copies of the resulting sixteen-page report, which is labeled as an INS record. She told me the FBI conducted the interrogation. She remembered the emphasis being about her stolen passport, with accusations that she had given it away or sold it. She recalled being asked if she knew the penalty for treason and being badgered for hours, with bright lights shining in her eyes the whole time. She was nearly hysterical by the time they concluded and was given a sleeping pill to calm her down.

The FBI indicated a desire to examine her; in a review of the case done in 1944, it is noted that the FBI questioned her at length. So there must have been two interrogations, although the FBI has been unable to find its records on either of my parents.

After a week of interrogations and hearings designed to "prove" that we Latin Americans were all entering the country illegally—thereby allowing indefinite detention—men, women, and children were put on a bus and driven to a railroad station. Authorities handed out identification numbers pinned on baggage tags that listed name and destination; we were to tie them to our clothing. Our tags read "Crystal City." At the station, we boarded a train and began the trip to Texas. The windows were dirty; no one could see out or see in.

Many of us children were now coughing so hard we had trouble catching our breath. Some, including Ingrid and me, began vomiting on the train as well. The illnesses begun during our stay at the German Club had been exacerbated by overcrowding and poor sanitary conditions on shipboard. After three days and four nights, we arrived in Crystal City, where a bus picked up our sick, exhausted families. We were driven through town—past the statue of Popeye that the city fathers had erected outside the courthouse to mark their town as the "spinach center of the world"—and into the barbed-wire gates of the camp. Our arrival is noted in camp records: February 12 at 3:00 PM.

In a small, red cardboard box, my father saved our numbered tags. I spread them out on my dining table. Each baggage tag has a large pin-on button with a number on it, except mine. Instead, I have a hand-numbered circle, made of cardboard. My tag is crumpled, stained, and spotted. I imagine I threw up on it.

"Immigration Detention Station, Terminal Island (San Pedro, California)" Endnotes

[1] Alien Enemy Control Unit Memo, 16 January 1943, DOJ Name Index File 146-13-2-1232, RG 60, NA.

[2] Warrants, 6 February 1943, DOJ Name Index File 146-13-2-1232, RG 60, NA.

[3] Board of Special Inquiry meeting, INS Service, BSI #13, 7 February 1943, from DOJ Name Index File 146-13-2-1232, RG 60, NA. Exclusion was based on three different statutes. Executive Order No. 8766 of May 22, 1918, Section 30 of Title III of the Act of June 28, 1940, and the Immigration Act of 1924.

[4] Sworn statement of Starr Pait Gurcke to Special Inspector Theron F. Culp at the immigration detention station, Terminal Island, California, 9 February 1943, DOJ Name Index File 146-13-2-1232, RG 60, NA, Washington D.C., 3. In a July 2000 email to me, Max Paul Friedman noted, "often an 'allegation' that there were 'Nazi meetings' was produced when an anonymous informant seeking payment from credulous US intelligence officers reported that he heard people getting together and speaking German in someone's home."

CRYSTAL CITY FAMILY INTERNMENT CAMP, TEXAS (1943–44)

According to Joseph O'Rourke's *Historical Narrative of the Crystal City Internment Camp*, in the fall of 1942, the Immigration and Naturalization Department established a family internment camp at the site of a former migrant-labor camp near Crystal City, Texas. Forty-one three-room cottages and one hundred and eighteen one-room shelters already existed there, as well as service buildings and sufficient utility services for the approximately two thousand people anticipated. The camp was originally intended to house only Japanese internees and their families, but temporary arrangements were made in December 1942 for thirty-five German families being transferred from Ellis Island and Camp Forrest, Tennessee, to Seagoville, which was not quite ready to receive them.

Our group of 131 Costa Rican deportees, as well as Germans from other Latin-American countries and the United States, arrived in February 1943. By March, more German families, as well as the first Japanese families, were interned. Additional Japanese were brought in from Camp Livingston, Louisiana, and Lordsburg, New Mexico. The first arrivals were expected to help with construction preparatory to housing more internees. The camp population in those early days was 378 Germans and 145 Japanese, but the number of prisoners soon mounted. O'Rourke wrote:

> From its inception through June 30, 1945, the Crystal City camp inducted 4,751 internees (including 153 births). Of this number, 954 Germans were repatriated in two movements (February 1944 and January 1945), and 169 Japanese were repatriated in August 1943. One hundred thirty-eight internees have been released or paroled, 84 interned at large, 73 transferred to other facilities, and 17 have died. In practically all cases, the women and children were voluntary internees.[1]

The Crystal City camp was considered the showplace of the internment program—so much so that the INS made a propaganda movie about it in the mid-1940s, showing families looking cheerful, relaxed couples lounging in their gardens, children and adults laughing in a crowded swimming pool, musicians and performers offering public entertainment, and children engaging in various school activities. Watching it now, one might believe the camp was a resort, not a prison.[2]

Medical facilities were primitive in the early days. According to O'Rourke, only one nurse was on staff when the first prisoners arrived in December. Happily, the camp employed more nurses, an internee physician, and volunteer aides when we and our fellow Costa Ricans arrived. "This group arrived with forty cases of whooping cough [pertussis] and an epidemic of impetigo. Fortunately, the camp was not yet crowded, and it was possible to isolate the entire party" (O'Rourke, 21).

Fifty-five children in our group were ill with whooping cough, according to a report on health care for interned enemy aliens published in the American Journal of Public Health in 2003. "Two children arrived with acute medical needs requiring immediate, outside hospitalization. Most of the adults suffered from severe respiratory ailments. In all, 66 needed immediate medical attention, and it was feared that others who manifested symptoms of simple colds might turn into medical cases."[3] Medical personnel examined us on February 13. Both my sister and I had whooping cough, while my mother was treated for bronchitis and possible whooping cough.

Our family was housed in one rather large room, with a double bed and a bunk bed for us girls at one end and a little corner stove at the other. There was a table to eat on, a couple of benches, and a few dishes. Toilets and bathing facilities were in another building down the road. My father took over the care of his family. He concocted meals from groceries that camp personnel brought to the door, cajoling and tempting his sick wife and daughters to eat. He changed and washed diapers. He filled buckets with water available at the bathroom, to heat for dishwashing and "cat baths" (sponge baths) for all his girls. My mother loved him for his efforts. If only she and we children weren't so miserable, she later told me, "being there alone together would have been heavenly."

Once we were all well, my family was moved to a newly built triplex; our unit had two small bedrooms and a kitchen-dining-living area with a kerosene stove with oven, running cold water and sink, and icebox. There was one toilet, to be shared with two other families. Communal bathing facilities were elsewhere (O'Rourke, 10). We were alone in the triplex until some time later, when a family from Brazil with one small girl moved into another unit. The couples shared child-care responsibilities with each other.

Furnishings for the triplex unit were bunk beds with sturdy rails to hold in sleeping children, a double bed, dining chairs and a table, and one wooden outdoor lounge chair. An initial allowance of cooking utensils, furniture, bedding, and so on was provided and could be replaced if the worn-out items were turned in. Nothing was very comfortable, but my parents no longer expected it to be. There was a war on, and everything they did had to do with that war. It was hard to remember their past life and impossible to imagine their future.

Photographs of our internment are few. At the time we were in Crystal City, no internee could have a camera. Authorities documenting camp prisoners took the most telling picture. It shows the whole family seated in front of a blank, white background. My mother is to the left, with Ingrid by her side; I stand beside my father. We children look wary, a little afraid. Ingrid seems to be pushing the photographer away with her hand, while I imitate her. My parents stare into the camera, their eyes dull, their faces haggard. My father is gaunt. He holds a cigarette in one hand. He smoked almost constantly by then.

At Crystal City, some semblance of order was restored in our lives. The internees were offered jobs for a salary of ten cents an hour. My father worked in a manufacturing division that constructed mattresses for the prisoners and was timekeeper for the maintenance division. He supplemented those hours by working with a

Crystal City, Texas Internment Camp maintenance division Werner, top row, far left, 1944

group dredging out an old reservoir full of water hyacinths and lining it with concrete. Internees were allowed to swim there as a reward for their labor. Working gave Werner back a sense of usefulness and helped lift the horrible sense of failure he felt for having been unable to protect and care for his family.

Charles sent checks on occasion, and friends sent money in lieu of gifts at Christmas. As always, my father kept meticulous records. (In his records, one sees that in the course of 1944, he found seventeen cents. Each penny is noted separately, with date found.) In March, the month after we arrived, he wrote, "I earned $5.80 (58 hours at 10 cents)." My parents were also able to take up to $30 monthly from personal funds.

Once we were deported, it became extremely difficult to access our accounts in Costa Rica. While interned, my mother wrote three times to Junta officials, but received no response. The officer in charge of the camp eventually wrote to the assistant commissioner for Alien Control, requesting that the office take "whatever action may be deemed appropriate" to help secure and protect Starr's property rights.[4] Apparently, my parents had decided that since my mother was a U.S. citizen, she might have more influence with the authorities than would my father. A note in his records shows that the Junta began sending checks to them in March 1944 and irregularly thereafter. In June 1947, the Junta still had $7,978.44 of their funds, which they never recovered.

My parents also began a campaign that was to take many years; they sought the return of a typewriter missing from their luggage after the USAT *Puebla* trip. My father wrote his first letter in May 1943, requesting that the Crystal City commanding officer look into the theft. Numerous forms, letters, and years later, Werner was reimbursed $64.50 by the Army on October 11, 1950. His struggle to reclaim the typewriter or get reimbursement seemed laughable to me as a child. Now I know the importance of that small victory after his years of loss, and his voluminous correspondence to various government agencies seems both poignant and courageous.

Originally, food was brought to our house. People outside the camp didn't have meat or had very little, while inside we were given too much. My mother actually had to throw out meat, because our little family could not eat it all, and the icebox was too small for storage. That first Christmas, my parents sent jam— overabundant in the camp and scarce out of it—to Charles and Virginia as a Christmas gift.[5]

A supervisor of education had been hired in April 1942 to plan the development of a school system. Setting up these schools and getting adequate teaching staff was a real challenge. Teachers fluent in English, Spanish, German, or Japanese were needed to work with the children. Both a German and a Japanese school were established, and by the autumn of 1943, an official school, based on Texas educational regulations, was in place for those students desiring an American education. Nursery schools and kindergartens were begun as soon as the camp opened and were run by the internees. My cousin Hermida, Karl Oskar and Pany's seventeen-year-old daughter, was a teacher's aide. (Later she became a nurse's aide and worked in the hospital.)

Numerous pictures from the camp show the children in German language preschool and kindergarten. Ingi and I are there, clinging to each other … but most striking is how *many* solemn-eyed children are pictured, all part of families whose lives have been shattered by the United States government's policies.

My sister and I were very excited—almost overwhelmed, at first—to be in "school" with so many other children. My parents noticed that Ingrid, voluble at home, hardly spoke in public. The most teachers could get out of her was "*Mich auch*" (me too) after I said something. We were inseparable, almost constantly holding hands. Was this usual, or were we frightened by our recent experiences? Ingi, in particular, was just beginning to use simple sentences and collect new words. Were the numerous languages she heard confusing her? My mother resolved to ask Liz or Virginia the next time she wrote. They both had children, and Liz, with an older daughter, always seemed to know the answers to mothering questions.

March 1944, Crystal City, Texas
A small number of the children in the German nursery school
front row, left: Ingrid with Heidi next to her

We had two visitors while imprisoned: my mother's brother, Charles; and Milton Morton, husband to my aunt Virginia's sister, Evelyn, and a lieutenant in the Medical Corp stationed at Camp Barkley, Texas. Charles, by then a physician with the communicable disease laboratory in the Los Angeles County General

Hospital, wrote a letter to the Crystal City authorities on March 23, 1943, asking for permission to visit.

In April, Charles arrived at the camp and was able to spend several days visiting with his sister under surveillance. He stayed elsewhere at night. Milton was not allowed to enter the camp during a visit sometime later, but my mother was able to see him briefly in an office, probably in a new visitation building that had been constructed near the main compound gate (O'Rourke, 14).

My mother tried to make our living area homier. At the time, there was one shared sewing machine available, and she made curtains. My father used apple crates to make bookcases and also built a back porch to our unit. We were across the dirt road from the barbed-wire fence, but looking beyond it, we could see miles and miles of gray-green brush and big, yellow black-eyed Susans. And at night there were stars, though the floodlights along the fence hampered our view. I remember the shadows those lights cast through the curtains in our bedroom.

The officer in charge noted, "Many improvements are effected … including the addition of porches and extra rooms by internees at their own expense, landscaping, gardening, etc. An estimated $50,000 have been spent by internees personally for this purpose" (O'Rourke, 12). But that was a report in mid-1945. While we were there, the area within the fences was bleak, with raw, new construction and dirt roads.

In their free time, my parents read books and magazines they bought and pored over Sears Roebuck and Montgomery Ward (nicknamed "Monkey Ward") catalogs. There was also a small library stocked with donated books. Charles sent them a radio, and occasionally outdoor movies were shown. My parents knew they were simply marking time, but they had no other option. And, at least for the moment, they were safe and together. Allowed to write to friends and family again, my mother resumed correspondence with her friend Liz.

Many of the German ladies walked the perimeter road each evening for their health, and sometimes my parents did too. But the walk, which ran along the ten-foot-high barbed-wire fence surrounding the compound, was depressing. There were towers with armed guards, and the view beyond was of desert. It vividly brought home that we were all prisoners. Since the camp only had a few hundred yards of all-weather roads originally, the walk was very dusty in the hot summer and muddy in the winter.

Dust devils danced through the camp in the summers—once swirling around Ingrid, terrifying her as she played on a swing. Another dust devil demolished the flimsy back porch our father had made. Grit seeped into the buildings, and the furniture of even the most dedicated housewives was filmed with dust. Scorpions, cockroaches, spiders, and biting red ants were frequent houseguests; outdoors, rattlesnakes were not uncommon. During the day, temperatures hovered well above one hundred degrees, on frequent occasions reaching one hundred and twenty; nights were not much cooler.

Hamburg, Germany, was bombed at the end of July 1943—not once, not twice, but repeatedly. Radio broadcasts told of horrific firestorms sweeping the city as fleets of British airplanes leveled neighborhood after neighborhood between July 24 and August 2. News reports indicated the city was almost completely destroyed, with an estimated thirty to fifty thousand civilians killed. There was no news of the senior Gurckes; there had been no letters for several years. My father was frantic but helpless. Sick with his imaginings, he passed the days in a trance, working by rote while he worried.

Finally, he and Karl Oskar received a Red Cross message—a few sentences, many months later—letting them know that their parents and brother had survived the bombings. My father remembered the hunger, the fear, the dreariness of war from his childhood. While he didn't know the details of his family's ordeal, his imagination supplied haunting images of the new horrors they must be facing. Thinking about his family and what they were experiencing gave him almost physical pain. Sometimes, especially at night, he could think of nothing else.

A new form of camp money was issued in September: coupon checks, a token system devised by camp officials to allow inmates to purchase needed foodstuffs or clothing items at a general store. Milk and ice continued to be delivered. My father was allotted six dollars' worth of coupons per month for our family. In 1944, the amount was raised to $6.50.

Now, with the token system in place, my mother was able to purchase just what our family needed, and there was no more wasted food. While food was plentiful, variety was limited. The first time Starr visited the store, she was suddenly struck with a clear memory of the San José *mercado* (market).

Closing her eyes, she could almost hear children's laughter, gossiping housewives, shouts of merchants hawking their wares, and flies buzzing in malodorous corners. For just a moment she could almost taste the fragrant sweetness of sugar cane *tapas* (coarse brown sugar cones) and ripe pineapples. How she missed the vivid piles of strange fruits and vegetables, slabs of beef and chicken carcasses heaped on tables, stacks of leather sandals, garlands of dried peppers, and colorful baskets of spices! A wave of intense homesickness engulfed her.

Security for the camp was provided by two sets of guards. A surveillance division patrolled the fence line and provided the armed guards for the towers, while an internal security division operated a small police force inside the compound twenty-four hours a day "to preserve order, count internees, and generally determine the state of affairs in the camp.... Very few internee fights or displays of violence have occurred. There have been no escapes or attempted escapes" (O'Rourke, 14–15).

The 1943–44 winter was the coldest Crystal City residents remembered. There was snow on the cacti, and scallops of ice formed on mud puddles. Rime patterned the barren ground and blackened grasses with frosted lace. We girls were fascinated with an icicle Papi brought into the house on a cracked brown plate. He'd broken it off the edge of our roof. We'd never seen nor tasted anything like it before.

In the first winters, mud was everywhere. The hospital, in particular, was surrounded with mud "practically up to the knees when it rained," and medical staff had to store extra clean shoes and stockings inside the building, to put on after they waded in and washed up (O'Rourke, 22).

At Christmas, Virginia and Charles sent both us girls overalls—the first we'd ever worn. From catalogs, our parents were able to order baby dolls and matching hand muffs (also shaped like dolls) for each of us. We even had a Christmas tree. A camp photographer took pictures of us seated in front of the tree at a small table our father built in the wood shop during free time.

For his wife, my father made a sewing box with multiple compartments for thread, pins, and so on. These forays into woodworking were his first and last. My mother was deeply touched by the effort. Her gift to him was a special dinner with some of his most loved foods: potatoes, of course, but made into one of his childhood favorites—large potato balls, which required what seemed like hours of grating; red cabbage simmered with a bit of bacon fat; and a small roast of pork. She even baked a cake.

When my father came home one winter evening, my mother told him about an appalling sight she'd seen that day; the teenage children of a Costa Rican family were walking barefoot outside in the snow, with their parents looking on. The teenagers were crying, the parents impassive. Some time later, my parents found out that the other adults insisted their children walk barefoot repeatedly in spite of the cold winter, to train for life in Germany. The family was looking forward to going back to Germany, and since the children had lived in the tropics all their lives, they had to prepare.

Many of the incarcerated Germans were nationalistic. A handful openly espoused Nazism. Recent experiences in their adopted countries and in the United States caused bitterness and predictably deepened feelings of alienation for some. Others simply preferred freedom to indefinite detention, even if it meant being sent to a war-torn country. Karl Oskar applied for repatriation to Germany for himself and his family as soon as it was offered.

Some of the Germans thought Germany was going to win the war, and they thought it would be over very soon. Neither of my parents believed that. When some of their fellow prisoners began to talk openly of their support for Hitler and of their belief that God was on Germany's side, Starr and Werner distanced themselves, associating with a few families that they considered "sensible." They were very careful to keep their mouths shut around the outspoken pro-Germans.[6] The couple wanted to win their freedom and move to the beach house in Santa Cruz, if and when that was allowed.

Karl Oskar's desire to return to Germany and his pro-Nazi attitude, as my father saw it, created an estrangement between the two brothers. Although the brothers' parents and younger brother harbored similar opinions, Werner felt less resentment toward them, believing that they were not able to get any information other than Nazi propaganda. Also, they were suffering through the unspeakable horror of another war.

Finally, on January 29, 1944, over one and a half years after his imprisonment had begun, my father's case was reviewed, and for the first time he was allowed to know and respond to the allegations against him.

"Crystal City Family Internment Camp, Texas (1943–44)" Endnotes

[1] Joseph L. O'Rourke, *Historical Narrative of the Crystal City Internment Camp*, a report to W. F. Kelly, assistant commissioner for Alien Control, Immigration and Naturalization Service, Crystal City Internment Camp, RG 85, 101/161, 32, NA, 8.

[2] *Alien Enemy Detention Facility*, Immigration and Naturalization Service, 1946. 16 mm videocassette, N3-85-86-1, NA, College Park, Maryland.

[3] Louis Fiset, DDS, BA, "Medical Care for Interned Enemy Aliens: a Role for the US Health Service in World War II," *American Journal of Public Health*, 2003 October; 93 (10): 1644–1654 (http://www.pubmedcentral.nih.gov/articlerender.fcgi?artid=1448029).

[4] J. L. O'Rourke, 17 September 1943 letter to assistant commissioner for Alien Control, INS internment camp file, RG 85, NA.

[5] O'Rourke, *Narrative*, notes that many of the staff were originally resentful that internees were being treated so well, and that this didn't "alleviate the general suspicions and accusations of a hostile public whose ration cards would not permit them to enjoy as much meat, sugar, etc., as nationals of enemy countries who were in government custody" (5).

[6] O'Rourke describes the difficulties staff and many of the interned Germans had with the original spokesperson chosen to represent them. He was "an individual thoroughly sold on his own importance and with a deep-seated Nazi philosophy … Life was soon miserable for most of the Germans in the camp …" The administration insisted another spokesperson be selected, but the former continued to use "underhand and terroristic methods" making the second spokesman "a puppet." After the second spokesman was repatriated to Germany in February 1944, a third person was chosen, who cooperated with the administration. The first spokesman and his family, as well as a number of others, were transferred to other camps during his tenure, easing tensions considerably (8–9).

THE CHARGES REVEALED

Three government programs interned civilians during World War II: the Alien Enemy Control Unit, the War Relocation Authority, and the U.S. State Department program in Latin America, which became known as the Special War Problems Division. Each targeted similar ethnic groups, using slightly different rationales, but none allowed those imprisoned to know the charges against them or to have legal counsel. The results of all three were the same: forcible removal from homes, family separations, loss of property and work, imprisonment for indefinite periods of time, and, in the case of Latin Americans, expulsion from chosen countries.

When people were picked up for internment in the United States under the Alien Enemy Control program, hearing boards convened to hear the charges. Francis Biddle, attorney general during this period, explained in later memoirs, "The hearings were informal, any 'fair' evidence could be admitted, and the alien could be represented by a relative or friend, but not by a lawyer—an exclusion that greatly expedited action, saved time, and put the procedure on a prompt and common-sense basis."[1]

Jerre Mangione, at the time in the public-relations department for the Immigration and Naturalization Service, wrote:

> Civil liberties took a back seat in those days; in the name of national defense expediency became the order of the day. The department's [Department of Justice] authority to "apprehend, detain or intern" any alien of enemy nationality for any reason whatsoever was based on an antiquated wartime law, the Alien Enemy Act of 1789 [sic].... Another inequity, authorized by the same act, was the department's disregard of due process of law in the procedures set up for the Alien Enemy Hearing boards. No alien appearing before the board could be represented by his attorney. The boards were not bound by any courtroom rules for establishing evidence; nor were they expected to submit a stenographic record of the testimony, which meant, in effect, that hearsay information carried far more weight than it should have.[2]

The approximately 120,000 Japanese Americans and resident Japanese imprisoned under the War Relocation Authority did not have even these cursory hearings at the beginning of their imprisonments. Neither did the Latin-American internees brought to the U.S. by the third, State Department program. Only at later review boards did these internees hear the charges that had devastated their lives.

Review-board members in Crystal City had access to a number of documents concerning my parents, many of them brief communiqués from the American Embassy in Costa Rica written by Lt. Col. Andino, the intelligence officer there. One of the earliest accusations came in 1941, in an FBI memo that stated "… a source generally reliable" had sent several reports naming Werner as possessing Nazi sympathies and claiming he was "one of the most dangerous German nationals in the country." Andino, who gathered the reports and sent them on to Washington, also labeled thirty-four other Costa Rican men as "most dangerous."[3]

Evidence offered to back these accusations included Werner and Starr's membership in the German Club and his stint as treasurer there during 1934–35. It was pointed out that before the war, my father contributed about five colones ($1) to the Winterhilfe (Winter Help), a benefit for Germans in need of assistance. Evidently, some of the money collected by that organization was used to fund Nazi Party work in Latin America during WWII. Werner also belonged to a local mutual benefit society, the Unterstützungverein, founded by Germans in Costa Rica in the early 1920s.

In June 1942, Andino submitted as further evidence a list of the names and addresses of businesses and individuals, some in foreign countries, found in Werner's possession. The FBI examined that list, and someone wrote "business" in pencil on it.

Lt. Col. Andino also pointed out that Werner was a distant relative of C. W. Lohrengel and originally worked for Lohrengel and Company. He wrote "C.W. Lohrengel not Nazi but insane. Son was pro-Nazi," in yet another report. In an additional memo, Andino insisted that my mother was "acting as dummy to cover Gurcke's commercial activities," and again asserted that Werner was dangerous. Apparently to Andino and U.S. authorities, these confused reports contained adequate evidence to justify my father's lengthy imprisonment and removal from Costa Rica.

The review-board members were favorably impressed with my father. They understood when he told them the Unterstützungverein was nonpolitical, focused purely on helping those in need. They knew similar societies had been formed by Italian groups in Latin America. In the written review of his case in Crystal City, they stated, "[Gurcke] stated that this organization had nothing to do with any political activities. It is probable that this ... is correct, inasmuch as such 'beneficencias' were organized by Italian and German groups throughout Latin-America prior to the advent of Hitler." His one donation to Winterhilfe was so small it hardly counted as support for the Nazi regime.

My father's explanation about the list of names and addresses jibed with the FBI comment on the side of the list. And the reason he kept his membership in the German Club seemed reasonable to the board.

When asked if he would fight in the United States Army, he said he would, though he preferred not to fight against Germany, because he had family there. He paused when asked if he would work in a munitions factory, then hesitatingly told them he could not, because his parents had recently been bombed out of Hamburg, and he could not make bombs that might be used against them.

He was firm when he told them he did not want to be repatriated to Germany. When they asked him to identify friends who were Nazis, he denied knowing any, and they understood his reluctance to name names.

The board members concluded that they would ask for the FBI report on my mother, Starr. If nothing detrimental showed up, they recommended we be released to internment at large.[4]

While the FBI report was pending, Karl Oskar was trying to be repatriated to Germany. When he saw that he, Pany, and Hermida were not on a list of Germans being sent in February 1944, he wrote to W. F. Kelly, assistant commissioner for Alien Control.

> My parents who reside in Hamburg, Germany were bombed out of their home during August of last year. My younger brother, their only child remaining in Germany, is in active service and therefore also not with them. I plead to be permitted to return to my beraved [sic] aging people who would be as grateful for having my moral as well as financial support, as I would be, if I could be allowed to render them this assistance.[5]

But as far as my parents knew, Üllie, the youngest brother, was not in the German military, because he had chronic stomach problems and poor eyesight. My father thought Ocki had lied in his letter to Kelly.

In February, my parents found out that we would probably be released on parole from the camp, but would not be able to settle in coastal areas, ruling out my mother's family home in California. My father also sent a letter to W. F. Kelly.

> The restriction "would seem to indicate that there is still some doubt in the minds of the authorities as to my loyalty to the United States and

my complete innocence of *any* Nazi activity whatsoever in the past.... In my case ... there was no reason whatsoever for my concentration in Costa Rica or my deportation, except my nationality. And that I intend to remedy by becoming an American citizen as soon as I am at liberty to do so. I can think of no reason now for the restrictions on my liberty except perhaps the action of my brother, Karl Oskar, in wanting to return to Germany. I can only say that in spite of being brothers we have always been entirely different in character and opinions and that I have *never* at any time shared his peculiar enthusiasm for the present German government. Before he left, he showed me a letter he had written to you asking for repatriation. He had written that he must get to Germany because his parents were aging and alone since his younger brother is in "active service." As I stated at my hearing, our younger brother is not in active service because of ill health, at least according to the most recent letters of our parents. My brother's outright lie has angered and worried me, and I sincerely trust it has not been the cause of the restrictions.[6]

My mother also wrote, adding her personal reasons for wanting parole to California.

> In California, where my friends know and like my husband and where our deportation from Costa Rica and internment here are known and understood, I feel certain our beginning a new life would be comparatively simple.... My brother visited me for a few days last year at this camp but I do not even know his children. My other relatives and friends I have not seen for six years and I am naturally most anxious to see them all again. This, I realize, is not a very valid reason, during a war when so many families and friends are separated ... but it deserves to be mentioned at least.[7]

Karl Oskar's request was granted, and he and his family joined the first group of Germans to be repatriated from Crystal City, sailing on the *Gripsholm* on February 11, 1944. Many dismal and difficult years passed before he and his family were able to return to Costa Rica.

My parents' hope for early release hinged on the results of the FBI report on my mother and a final reevaluation by the chief of the review section. In April, a summary of the findings was sent to the chief by an unidentified source (probably FBI) concluding that the board's recommendation should be denied. The chief decided to accept the original recommendation and scrawled "relaxed internment" on the summary.[8] (The term "relaxed internment" was soon changed to "internment at large" in official documents, when it was decided that the former term connoted circumstances much too pleasant for prisoners.)

On May 2, 1944, Francis Biddle, attorney general of the United States, signed an order allowing "said enemy alien [to] be interned within an area within the continental limits of the United States under the supervision of the Immigration and Naturalization Service."[9] California was not off-limits. The next day, my mother's arrest warrant was canceled "Inasmuch as it appears that this subject is a native-born citizen of the United States."[10]

Once my parents were given a date for their release, they began to think about their future. For so long, they had simply sleepwalked through the days. They tried not to get too excited, but as the day of departure came closer, my mother became increasingly anxious. She didn't think she and Werner could bear it if for some reason they weren't freed.

While they made sure we children had new clothes, they themselves looked shabby and threadbare. Prior to release, each was issued a pair of shoes from camp stocks; my mother got a dress and a coat ("dowdy but serviceable," she told me years later), and my father, new slacks and a shirt.

On May 22, my father officially became an internee at large, and at 4:00 that afternoon we were driven to the train station in Uvalde. There we were given tickets to Santa Cruz and the beach house, by train and bus, with an allowed layover in Los Angeles, California, where we would spend a few days with Charles and his family.

Until the train pulled away from the station, my parents were barely able to breathe. They held us in their arms so tightly that we both began to squirm and complain—first quietly, then more and more loudly in German.

My parents were embarrassed and frightened. How would fellow passengers react to a family with children who spoke no English, only *German*? They did their best to shush us up and managed for quite a while by telling stories and playing games. But we eventually tired of quiet; wriggling free, we ran around, commenting on everything and everyone.

Finally, a woman across the aisle, who'd been watching and listening intently, asked my father if he were an ambassador or somehow connected to an American legation in Germany. He took a deep breath and told her "yes" in as dignified and unaccented English as he could muster. My mother quickly stepped in, and when the woman's curiosity was satisfied, she turned back to Werner, who rolled his eyes. That set her off in nervous giggles, which she smothered as quickly as she could.

My parents were able to relax only after they finally calmed us down and tucked us into a berth. Then they sat in silence, holding hands, watching mile after glorious mile slip by.

"The Charges Revealed" Endnotes

1 Francis Biddle, *In Brief Authority* (New York: Doubleday & Company Inc., 1962), 208.

2 Jerre G. Mangione, *An Ethnic at Large: A Memoir of America in the Thirties and Forties* (New York: G. P. Putnam's Sons, 1978), 284.

3 FBI Memo, undated, DOJ stamp 30 October 1943, Alien Enemy Unit, DOJ Name Index File 146-13-2-1232, RG 60, NA. Also, see Bell to Ennis, 7 December 1943, file 711.5, Costa Rica Confidential File, Box 26, RG 84, stack 350, 53/27/5, NA. Assigned by Edward J. Ennis, head of the Alien Enemy Control Unit, Raymond Ickes and James D. Bell, young Spanish-speaking lawyers, reviewed the allegations and evidence for U.S. intervention in Latin-American arrests and deportations in 1943. Bell, looking over Costa Rican files for 143 internees, concluded that in the case of the 35 prisoners considered "most dangerous," "… there was no evidence whatsoever" against 14 of them. In 15 other cases, there were perhaps only one or two allegations of possible merit. "… in only 6 cases was the evidence on these 'most dangerous individuals' sufficient to classify them as a genuine threat."

4 January 29, 1944, Report on Hearing at Crystal City, Texas, DOJ Name Index File 146-13-2-1232, RG 60, NA.

5 Karl Oskar Gurcke, letter to W. F. Kelly, assistant commissioner for Alien Control, 6 February 1944, INS Internment Camp File 146-13-2-1583, RG 85, NA.

6 Werner Gurcke, letter to W. F. Kelly, assistant commissioner for Alien Control, 16 February 1944, INS Internment Camp File 146-13-2-1232, RG 85, NA.

7 Starr Gurcke, letter to W.F. Kelly, assistant commissioner for Alien Control, 16 February 1944. INS Internment Camp File 146-13-2-1232, RG 85, NA.

8 April 26, 1944, memorandum for the chief of the Review Section, DOJ Name Index File 146-13-2-1232, RG 60, NA.

9 Francis Biddle, attorney general, Order in the Matter of Werner Gurcke, Alien Enemy, DOJ Name Index File 146-13-2-1232, RG 60, NA.

10 Edward J. Ennis, Director, memorandum for Willard F. Kelly, assistant commissioner for Alien Control, DOJ Name Index File 146-13-2-1232, RG 60, NA.

INTERNMENT AT LARGE

In our albums, there are many pictures of life at the beach house: Ingrid and I, with our friends, line the steps to the front porch, smiling, tousled, arms linked; my father holds us by the hand as we prance in the waves at the beach; all of us sit under another Christmas tree, in a sea of wrappings. In early views of my parents, they appear younger and less drawn than they had in the camp, but their gaze is distant, and their eyes are sad.

We spent several days in Los Angeles with Charles and Virginia and their two children, John and Barbara, before traveling by train and bus to Santa Cruz. We had supper at a small café in the center of town and then took a taxi to the Seabright beach house.

The house seemed like a castle. There was so much room compared to the triplex in Crystal City. There was comfortable, upholstered furniture; a real kitchen, dining, and living room; and two bedrooms upstairs. My father held my mother in his arms while her tears spilled over. At last, we had a home again.

We girls had never seen such a wondrous place. Chairs that were soft! Stairs to climb! A toilet in the house! So many rooms! Oblivious to our parents' emotions, we explored the house—peering into closets, bouncing on furniture, racing up and down the stairs, and constantly tugging at our parents to "come see."

In the days that followed, my parents took great long walks. It seemed unbelievable to them to have so much space. They walked for miles, turning around only when we children were too tired. Papi often carried Ingrid on his shoulders, so we could go just a little farther. My mother told me both she and my father could not get enough of their marvelous freedom. Some days the air smelled of sea spray, fog, and eucalyptus; other days were scented with pine needles, sunshine, and roses. My father began to lose his haunted look.

We had exactly $1,333.23 when we left Crystal City. On June 5, my father received a check of $11.50 for work he had done at the camp. Moneys from Costa Rica continued to trickle in, to their amazement. After all, those debts could so easily have been ignored.

My father began looking for work right away and was hired almost immediately by a Mexican labor-camp supplier, because he spoke fluent Spanish. He bought groceries, like sides of beef and crates of vegetables, and delivered them to various labor camps in a small truck. He earned $250 a month, which seemed a fortune to my parents. His duties soon expanded to planning menus and supervising health regulations. The Mexican laborers in these camps worked in the fields, replacing U.S. workers who were in the military or Japanese-American farmers who were still imprisoned. The lonely farm workers, isolated from their families in Mexico, welcomed my father, and when he occasionally brought Ingrid and me, they coddled us, giving us treats bought especially for us.

My father's work gave him enormous satisfaction. At least now he could provide for his family. Gradually, he allowed himself to think of a future where he was free. He wanted to begin another importing business when restrictions were lifted on contacting foreign companies. He hoped it would be in Costa Rica.

By the end of June, a local businessman agreed to sponsor him, meeting with him weekly and overseeing his actions. Now, mandated weekly reports he wrote to an INS office in Salinas were reduced to twice monthly.

Most neighbors, remembering my mother and her parents, welcomed us. More than one neighbor offered to take pictures of the family or of us children playing, since my parents were still not allowed a camera. Relatives and old friends came to visit and to proffer any help they could.

However, one neighbor was openly hostile, calling the local police frequently to complain that Ingrid and I played too noisily, talked "in a foreign language," and were, all in all, nuisances. Each time, an officer would apologetically knock on the door to let my parents know, but also told them not to worry about it. They *did* worry, though, and always cautioned us to walk and talk quietly while playing on the porch—an admonition rarely heeded for long. (In May 1945, the INS again investigated my father and interviewed a police officer who stated that the neighbor "was frankly a neighborhood crank; that she had called the police on numerous occasions; that each call is investigated but not recorded as to date they have never found anything justifying action."[1])

Those were happy times for Ingrid and me. Seemingly endless summer days were spent at the beach; we learned to dog-paddle, make drip castles, and—quite easily—speak English. We went to bed sandy, salty, satisfied. There were neighborhood bonfires on the weekends and monthly outdoor dances. My father learned to sing the chorus of songs like "Oh My Darling, Clementine" and "By the Beautiful Sea," and delighted us by dancing with my mother and the two of us.

Both parents took turns reading to us from books borrowed from the library, just a block away. Daily trips to the local grocery, variety store, and post office were adventures too. A cold-water tap outdoors served to rinse off sand, but bath nights were held in the kitchen, where a large, galvanized steel tub was filled with water warmed on the stove. While one of us was bathed, the other drew pictures on the steamy kitchen windows.

Although my parents felt freer, they soon realized they were not really secure. My father needed permission to travel anywhere out of the county. United States government policies regarding internment at large were incomplete, and changes were made from month to month. Mail was censored. Secret investigations into their activities continued, and their status as "at large" was questioned.

Officials at the U.S. Embassy in Costa Rica felt the internees at large were being treated too leniently, which might damage their agency's credibility. They also were concerned that continued pursuit of more deportations, now being used to remove German businesses and replace them with American concerns, might be hampered.[2]

When the Department of State sent United States embassies in Latin America a request to evaluate the internees at large—in particular, the possibility of deleting some of them from the Proclaimed List—the Costa Rican response was sent in an airgram dated August 26 and signed by Fay Allen Des Portes, the U.S. ambassador at the time.

> The Embassy strongly feels that it is inadvisable to recommend at this time the deletion of any of the proclaimed [sic] List nationals who are presently "interned at large", not only because it is felt there is sufficient evidence to retain the names on the Proclaimed List, but because of the difficulties which would be encountered locally in explaining the reason for such deletion.... It is further felt that the continuance of those persons in an "internment at large" status can only reflect unfavorably upon the Proclaimed List in Costa Rica inasmuch as the relatives and friends of the persons concerned are already well aware of their status and ... the economic position of all of the "internees at large" from Costa Rica is undoubtedly better than it ever was here where for example the average wage for manual labor is less that $1.00 per day and where white collar workers receive average salaries ranging between $40.00 and $110.00 per month.

Ambassador Des Portes went on to summarize the case against seven deportees, including my father, and stated that another report about other deportees would follow.[3] On the advice of the Department of Justice, four internees at large were again arrested, while my father and two others were allowed to continue on parole.[4]

F. O. Seidle, the chief of the Alien Control Division of the INS, sent periodic letters that informed alien enemies of additional requirements. My parents had to use internee-of-war forms for any letters written, and the return address was to be "in care of Alien Control Officer, Immigration and Naturalization service" in San Francisco, the office that also read over all mail before it could be sent. The official Christmas card was titled in German, and only one package, not over four pounds, could be sent to Latin-American destinations.

In winter, the little beach house rocked and groaned as storm winds blew. The sounds of crashing waves and a lusty buoy filled many days and nights; at other times, the sea swirled to shore with gentle hisses, and the air was bright blue and gold. We combed the beach on sunny winter days looking for shells and driftwood. Ingrid and I soon decorated the steps to the porch with colorful seaweed, bits of shell, rocks, and other treasures. And our parents continued to take long walks, rain or shine, reveling in their freedom.

As Christmas drew nearer, my parents delighted in plans to make the holiday as magical as possible for us. After we were put to bed, they spent happy hours talking about the Christmas traditions in each of their childhood families, choosing what to pass along. I, after all, was now four, and Ingrid three. This would be the first Christmas we might remember. (And I have, though what I describe below may actually be a mix of several Christmases.)

Festivities began several days early, when Das Weinachtsmann (Father Christmas) secretly visited the house to find out if we'd been good. He left a trail of sparkling artificial snow, which we found the next morning. On Christmas Eve he came again, greeted by my father while the rest of us were upstairs. Magically, it seemed, a music-box melody began to play, and a deep voice asked, "*Sein Sie alle artig?*" "*Ya, ya,*" everyone replied. We *had* been good. Rushing downstairs after Santa left, we found not only books, toys, candy canes, and tangerines, but also an amazing new piece of furniture: a phonograph player that our father bought for our mother. While we listened to Bing Crosby sing "White Christmas," our mother gave our father a bottle of their favorite orange liqueur—one that must have brought back bittersweet memories of Costa Rica.

The precariousness of their situation was driven home a week later, on January 2, 1945. My father came home from work to find he'd received a personal letter from Mr. Seidle of Alien Control. Momentarily, he was flooded with hope, but as he read, his spirits plummeted.

Dear Sir:

The Department of Justice has ordered that your internment at large has been restricted to other than coastal areas in the United States, and that you will be given 30 days from date hereof in which to comply with the order. Also, you are advised that it has been made a condition of your internment at large that you not accept any employment which is connected with the importing and exporting business. Transportation to your new place of residence will be furnished by the government. For your information, the West Coast Defense Area includes the State of California and the western half of the States of Washington and Oregon. Please inform this office promptly of your plans so that the necessary arrangements may be made.

My parents stayed up late into the night trying to plan, trying to think of a way we might be allowed to remain in Santa Cruz. My father despondently wrote back the next day. "Will you please advise me whether we are permitted to go to Nevada or Arizona. We have no friends or connections in either state, but I am doing my best to find out something about the possibilities of employment, etc. Will adequate housing be found for us? We have two small children."

When my father told his employer, Ramón Fernández, that he was to be forced to relocate, Mr. Fernández also wrote, requesting an interview with Mr. Seidle. He valued Werner as an employee and had realized quickly that the reasons for his internment had little merit. He promised Werner to do his best to arrange work for him wherever he was transferred. On the tenth, after Mr. Fernández's interview with Mr. Seidle, my father's boss wrote again to Mr. Seidle to clarify my father's job description and to assure INS that there was no import or export business being done.

As suddenly as the threat of being uprooted appeared, it was canceled without explanation on January 15, 1945. Mr. Seidle signed the letter "for the District Director." "The order for your removal from the Pacific Coast area has been rescinded and you may remain in your present employment."

The cancellation did little to lift my father's spirits. Still completely at the mercy of others, he felt almost as trapped and hopeless as he had in the prison in Costa Rica. There seemed to be no end to his family's difficulties. He'd been given the name of an American Civil Liberties Union lawyer in San Francisco who might be able to help us, but without transportation, seeing him would be difficult. Instead, he made contact with Stewart Cureton, a lawyer living in our neighborhood, who tried to find a legal solution to the limbo my father was in. Uneasily, my parents settled into a routine of work, family, and friends, determined that my sister and I would have as normal and happy a childhood as they could manage for as long as it was allowed.

U.S. government policies shifted abruptly over the months that followed. The Junta de Custodia sporadically sent small checks made out to the Immigration and Naturalization Service from the Banco Nacional de Costa Rica, and it was necessary to have the checks endorsed by the financial officer at the Crystal City camp. But in February, my parents had a check returned to them from Crystal City, because "it is believed that the government would become a party to the transaction if this [endorsement] were done." The check had to be returned to Costa Rica to be reissued—problematic at best.

Letters, which my mother had been writing on internee-of-war stationery, were suddenly returned in March 1945 with a note from Mr. Seidle: "We can find nothing in our regulations that international mail written by relatives of internees-at-large must be censored by this Service." By August, it was no longer necessary for my father to use a special form for his letters.

But being an alien enemy did not exempt him from the draft. He had signed up willingly with the draft board in Zavala County, Texas, hoping to demonstrate his allegiance to the United States, and had been classified IIB. (All male internees of eligible age had to register.) In August 1944 and again in April 1945, that classification was changed to IA, a designation that meant the possibility of immediate call-up to service. Ramón Fernández, my father's boss, intervened both times. He was able to convince the board that my father's work was essential to the war efforts, and his draft classification was changed to IIA. (IIA and IIB indicated deferred status.)

The couple could hardly believe that Werner was classified IA, even briefly. It was almost laughable. He was considered so dangerous that he had been imprisoned for nearly two years, such a threat that he was forced to leave his chosen country and his livelihood. How could it be that the United States wanted him to serve in the U.S. military? As with Alice's stay in Wonderland, life just got curiouser and curiouser.

By then, my parents had saved enough money to purchase a small used car. Thrilled to have even more mobility, they planned outings and took us on regular family drives on Sunday. We were picnicking in the town square of San Juan Bautista the day the war with Germany ended. As mission bells chimed, my mother cried with joy. My parents must have thought that their long ordeal was over.

"Internment at Large" Endnotes

[1] Kelly to Clattenburg, 16 July 1945 with INS Report of Investigation, 28 May 1945, 711.62115 AR/7-1645, Box 40, State Department Central Decimal Files, 1945–49.

[2] See Friedman, *Nazis and Good Neighbors*, 171–76, for a full account of the expropriation policies; also Carlos Calvo Gamboa, *Costa Rica en la Segunda Guerra Mundial (1939–1945)* (San José, Costa Rica: Editorial Universidad Estatal a Distancia, 1985), 41–51.

[3] American Embassy, San José, Costa Rica airgram of August 26, 1944. Box 40, Records of the Special War Problems Division, NA. For more information on Des Portes and the United States' continued efforts to deport more Germans from Costa Rica, see Friedman, *Nazis and Good Neighbors*, 176–82.

[4] D. G. Tenney, Confidential Review, 711.62115 AR/1-2146, Box 40, State Department Central Decimal Files, 1945–49.

FORCED REPATRIATION?

Buoyed by the news of the war's end, my parents seriously began to consider their plans for the future. If my father were to begin another import business, where should it be? My mother admitted that she'd like to stay in the United States. Ingrid and I seemed happy and secure, and since my parents had always intended for us to go to college here, it seemed to her that it was better simply to remain.

Papi's feelings were more complicated. He loved Costa Rica and really longed to return, when and if he were able. But he was still considered an enemy alien and, until that label was lifted, his future remained unsettled.

A Department of State press release was sent to all internees in November 1945, regarding "the disposition" of enemy aliens brought to the United States from other American republics. Many had been repatriated, but there remained "a considerable number of others, including many who were leaders in anti-American activities, [who] now decline to return to their native countries, wishing to move back to Latin America or to remain here."

The press release mentioned a meeting of all American republics at a conference in Mexico City the prior year that included a recommendation for measures "'to prevent any person whose deportation was deemed necessary for reasons of security of the Continent from further residing in this Hemisphere, if such residence would be prejudicial to the future security or welfare of the Americas.' Pursuant to that recommendation, on September 8 the president of the United States [Harry S. Truman] by Proclamation [2662] authorized the Secretary of State to order the repatriation of dangerous alien enemies deported to this country during the war."

The press release went on: "In proceeding with this program the Department intends to follow an orderly procedure wholly consistent with American concepts of fairness and equity." Cases were to be reviewed "with a view to releasing as quickly as possible those persons who may safely be allowed to remain in this Hemisphere."[1]

Further information was sent in January. Three Latin-American countries refused to allow the State Department to decide the future of the aliens deported from their countries. They were requesting the return of some, or all of those deported. Other countries were requesting the return of specific individuals. Therefore, the State Department decided that countries must either accept all their aliens back and assume full responsibility for them or allow the United States government to continue primary responsibility and decision-making. Pending word on each country's choice, cases would continue to be reviewed.

This January 1946 bulletin sent by the State Department answered the question "By what authority am I being held in custody?" with the following explanation:

> You are being held in custody under the authority of the Alien Enemy Act (Sections 4067 4070 of the Revised Statutes of the United States) which gives the President of the United States power to confine and deport natives or citizens of an enemy country in time of war. You will note that a state of war still exists between the United States and its enemies, since no peace has yet been signed.[2]

Also in January, a confidential report by D. G. Tenney, who reviewed the government files on many of the internees, including my parents, stated, "There have been loose allegations to the effect that Mrs. Gurcke was pro-German and 'dangerous' but ... the allegations are not supported by any evidence or specific charges," and concludes "Gurcke should be released for lack of evidence of Nazi activity or sympathy."[3]

February 25, 1946, was an eventful day. The mailman, on his first delivery of the day, brought notice from the INS that "all alien enemy proceedings have been canceled in your case." This was good news, but my parents were wary—with good reason. When my father answered a knock on the door later the same day, Lowell W. Hoffer, an immigrant inspector, handed him a warrant for his arrest.

Because Werner had entered the country without an unexpired passport or other travel documents "showing his origin and identity ... it appears that the alien ... has been found in the United States in violation of the immigration laws thereof, and is subject to be taken into custody and deported ..." Mr. Hoffer then gave him another paper, an order of parole, allowing him to "remain at large" under the supervision of the INS.

The charge of illegal entry was being used to deport the prisoners once more—this time to the countries of their ethnic origins, not the countries of their choosing. Again threatened with separation and the loss of their home, Starr and Werner despaired of ever being free.

Advised that a hearing of his case would be conducted in the Salinas office of INS in March, my father was told that he could have counsel if he wished, and that he was to bring, in triplicate, copies of his marriage license and the birth certificates of his wife and children.

In the meantime, eighteen neighbors, learning of my father's possible repatriation, signed a petition to the U.S. Department of Justice testifying that his "conduct and moral character ... have been above reproach. He has been an active, self-reliant member of our community, an excellent neighbor ... a devoted husband and father ... and it is our firm belief that his deportation and separation from his family would result in serious hardship for himself, his wife and children, and deprive us of an intelligent, cultured, responsible resident."

The hearing was held, but a decision was left pending. While he waited, my father wrote to various business associates and friends asking for recommendations to bolster his request to remain in the United States. He also made a momentous decision; he would begin an export/import business of his own in the United States. Getting back to Costa Rica was an unrealistic dream. And if he were sent to Germany, perhaps his wife could run the business until he was somehow able to return.

For months, he had been thinking about the type of product he could import or export. After investigation, and at the counsel of friends, he made contact with Spanish suppliers of Portuguese cork, which he theorized could become a growing necessity for the fledgling wine industry in California.

On March 1, 1946, Werner resigned his position with Ramón Fernández's firm and struck out on his own. The business began slowly, and to his chagrin he needed to supplement it with another job. He worked in a local cannery, volunteering for the night shift so that he would have the days free for his business. He also admitted to my mother that he was embarrassed to be working at such a menial position and hoped the neighbors wouldn't see him.

His German accent was strong, but his English by that time was very good. The owners or overseers he spoke to at the wineries were often first- or second-generation Italians with accents of their own, and that seemed to create a bond. And, of course, many had experienced at least some difficulties as enemy aliens during the war. Because my father was pleasant, persistent, and completely reliable, his business grew.

Each summer Papi took us children, one at a time, on one of his business trips. Cool coastal air would evaporate as we drove through the heat-filled day to the Napa Valley. His left arm was toasted brown from resting on the window frame of the car. There was no air-conditioning, and dry, hot wind swirled through the car while I fidgeted, bare legs sticking to the Naugahyde seat, hair blowing into my mouth and eyes. In the back of the car were bales of corks bagged in rough and fragrant burlap.

The wineries were a wonderful relief, because we usually went into the cellars while my father did business. Cool and dark, the cellars smelled of fruit and fermentation. Huge casks loomed in shadowy corners. I leaned against the walls, trying to soak in that coolness before we had to go. If we were lucky, they would offer us some grapes or juice, or—less satisfactorily from my point of view—a taste of wine.

The end of the day was my favorite. We'd check into a small hotel, and I would immediately look into the bathroom, hoping for a bathtub. While Papi wrote up his notes for the day, I could be a mermaid, blowing diamond bubbles in the bathwater; or dream of being Esther Williams, pointing one leg elegantly toward the ceiling while trying to smile open-eyed underwater. Then it was time to go to a restaurant, just he and I. The heat of the day would fade to a comfortable warmth while we ate and talked. After that, we might go to a movie or go back to the hotel to call my mother, then read until it was bedtime.

One sunny summer day in 1946, Werner received a letter from his mother— the first news of his family since 1943. After my mother shooed us outside to play, my parents sat down at the round, wooden dining table to read it. The news was terrible: his Aunt Olga, one of Frieda's sisters, burned to death in the *Brandkatastrophe* (firestorm) which followed the July and August 1943 bombings of Hamburg. When Max and Frieda were able to return to their neighborhood after the bombings, their home was gone, as were those of all their relatives. They had camped in the ruins, collecting what little there was to salvage, and then moved to the city's outskirts, where they struggled daily to survive in the chaos.

But worse news followed. Ülrich, my father's youngest brother, was finally conscripted into the military, though sickly. He died when a hand grenade exploded during training exercises in February 1945. He was twenty-five.

Ülrich married mid-September the year before. We have one photograph. Üllie is solemn, as are the fathers who flank the young couple. His bride, Dorothea, is dressed in a trench coat and holds flowers. She is smiling. Not five months later, she will be a widow.

Werner's father, too, was dead, less than a month after Üllie and just two months before Germany's surrender. Max refused to eat after Üllie's death and died "of a broken heart." Karl Oskar and his family were as well as could be expected, as was his mother, Frieda.

When we tired of play, we returned to find our father crying. I had never seen him cry before and was both surprised and dismayed. His sorrow seemed to seep into me. I became obsessed with loss, reading obituaries as best I could and listening to the radio for stories of disaster—always in plentiful supply.

At dinner one evening not long after the letter, I looked up the darkened stairwell and saw what I now believe was a child's imagined version of death. As I became increasingly hysterical, incoherent and sobbing, my frightened parents, unable to calm me, finally called our doctor. He came as quickly as he could, to find me wild-eyed, screaming that a wolf was coming down the stairs in a cloud of darkness to take me away.

Over the next years, I had frequent nightmares. In all of them, a wolf enveloped me in a twilight gloom so complete that my family disappeared, vanished forever. Gradually, as I grew, the nightmares faded, but my memory of that vision remains vividly clear.

The hearing over my father's repatriation was continued in December of that year. My mother was to be present; her testimony might be taken. By then, my father had rounded up numerous letters testifying to his moral conduct and good behavior from U.S. and Costa Rican sources. He had also filled out the necessary government form—an application for suspension of deportation.

Six months later, a copy of the proposed findings was sent to my parents. They were given ten days to file any exceptions. The findings were then to be forwarded to Philadelphia for review and a final decision. In the findings, the Immigration and Naturalization Service's charges against my father were laid out, primarily concerning "illegal entry" into the United States.

"As respondent's stay was to be for an indefinite period, necessarily so due to the belief that his surveillance was in the interest of national safety for the duration of the last war," he was considered an immigrant at the time of entry. As such, based on the Immigration Act of May 26, 1924, he was an immigrant without valid visa. He was also found to have entered the United States without a passport "of the country to which he owes allegiance or other travel document showing his origin and identity," an action made illegal by the Passport Acts of May 22, 1918, and February 5, 1917.

The "Proposed Conclusion of Law" was "that under Section 20 of the Immigration Act of 1917, the respondent is deportable to Germany at government expense."

However, there were factors allowing for discretion in the ruling. "He is of the white race" was the first mitigating circumstance. His marriage to an American citizen was noted, as were his children, along with the fact that he had worked steadily since being released from Crystal City.

> He has produced evidence of his good moral character prior to his entry into the United States and it has been established beyond a reasonable doubt that he has been a person of good character since his entry except for the period of approximately 14 [sic] months prior to May 22, 1944, during which period he was interned as an enemy alien.

There is no showing in the record that respondent, during the period of his internment, was other than a person of good moral character, or that he had behaved in a manner which would indicate that he believes and adheres to any totalitarian form of government. There appears to be no indication that respondent has ever been a fanatical follower of the former Nazi Party if at all.

The "Conclusion of the Law" was that Werner was "eligible for suspension of deportation," and that is what Robert H. Lowry, the presiding inspector, recommended. My parents crossed their fingers and waited while the decision was being reviewed in Philadelphia.

(It is interesting to note that while my father and other Latin-American deportees in the United States struggled to avoid being sent to Germany, and the United States continued to pressure Latin-American countries to repatriate all Germans, the U.S. government began a then top-secret program, called Operation Paperclip, designed to bring *into* the United States Nazi Germany's top scientists and engineers. Fifty to eighty percent of them were former Nazi Party members … and some, like Klaus Barbie, known as the butcher of Lyon, were guilty of war crimes.[4])

While my parents waited for the review and decision, family and work occupied them. Ingrid and I were now in elementary school. The little beach house that once seemed so spacious was cramped and small for a growing family. Since my father's cork-import business was doing well, he no longer had to supplement his income with cannery work. My parents began to dream of a new home and to hope for another child. My mother was thirty-six; my father thirty-nine.

On December 17, 1947, they received a copy of the final decision: "If Congress takes no action adverse to the order granting suspension of deportation, and when the required fee is paid, proceedings [will] be canceled."

"If Congress takes no action …" meant more waiting. Congress did not change the order. On July 29, 1948, word came that for a fee of $18 a record of lawful entry would be created, paving the way for permanent residence. My father mailed a postal order the next day.

In October, we moved to a larger home just a few blocks away from the beach house. At last, on October 29, 1948, INS official Robert Lowry sent my father a letter stating that as of the twelfth his deportation was suspended, his arrest warrant was canceled, and a record indicating lawful entry into the country had been created. The commissioner of the INS, Watson B. Miller, also sent a letter concluding, "I extend best wishes for your success in your new country."

To Starr and Werner's delight, my mother gave birth to their first son, my brother Karl, two weeks later on November 14.

A few years later, María, our Costa Rican neighbor, finally sent the large, wooden trunk she had had made, packed with the special items my parents wanted to keep. Though the items were chosen with haste during that brief, difficult time in the days before deportation, they remembered some of the things with great fondness. Our parents excitedly called us to the garage. Here were their books, photograph albums, some baby clothes and toys, and household linens—a trunk full of memories of another place and time.

As the trunk opened, the smell of mildew permeated the air. Nothing had escaped the damp and warmth. Linens wore stains of green and dark gray. Cloth bindings sagged on favorite books while inside pages stuck together, rippled and marked with moisture. Many photographs were blotched and faded, the cobweb marks of the albums' separating papers swirling over landscapes and obliterating faces. The only photographs my parents had been able to take of Ingrid as a baby, before their camera was confiscated, were gummed together and most tore when they tried to separate them. These last few, most cherished of possessions had become further casualties of the war that had taken so much from them.

"Forced Repatriation?" Endnotes

[1] F. O. Seidle, chief, Detention, Deportation, and Parole Section, Department of State Press Release, 2 November 1945, No. 826. Also, Presidential Proclamation No. 2662, 8 September 1945.

[2] Department of State memorandum, 4 January1946, sent to Latin-American governments and also all internees from Latin America, along with a five-page bulletin summarizing the memorandum and "answers to commonly asked questions."

[3] D. G. Tenney, Confidential Review, 711.62115 AR/1-2146, Box 40, State Department Decimal Files, 1945–59.

[4] Friedman, *Nazis and Good Neighbors*, 226.

HOME AT LAST

Why did my parents stay in the United States rather than return to Costa Rica once it was possible?

My father was not free to consider returning to Costa Rica until the end of 1948, over five years after he'd been forcibly removed. He would have had to abandon his cork-import business in California and begin other work once again, a prospect that must have seemed daunting. My mother was pregnant and about to deliver their third child. And many years later, she told me that having their children become American citizens had always been a goal, because "it seemed to be the most solid kind of citizen to be; certainly it was in those days."

Starr, Karl, and Werner-Summer 1950
Seabright Beach, Santa Cruz, California

On April 21, 1952, my father became a naturalized citizen of the United States. Walter Pait, my mother's uncle, wrote in his diary, "Went to the superior [sic] Court at 10 a.m.—as witness and to recommend Mr. Werner Gurcke for a citizen of the U.S. of America. He passed in the shortest time of any applicant of the 33 who tried."

For my mother, California was home. But my father, though he never spoke of it to us children, had painfully mixed feelings. While he knew it was common sense to stay in Santa Cruz, he often longed for Costa Rica. In the summer of 1955, he took a trip alone to visit his mother in Hamburg and business associates in Spain. He then spent some time in Costa Rica. He wrote long letters to his wife and to us describing his experiences.

Werner realized almost immediately that he was no longer German in any way. He tried to talk to his mother and others about the war, but "According to Mino [his mother] and probably lots of others, Hitler and the Germans are not to blame at all.... so I prefer to shut my mouth before we come into arguments about it." The rigidity of the culture made him nervous; certain clothes had to be worn, certain gifts brought when visiting, certain customs observed. His mother was even critical of his short-sleeved shirts—unsuited for wear in Hamburg, she said, because they were "cowboy clothes." The only place in Hamburg where he felt really comfortable was at the home of his aunt Annchen, who had been to Costa Rica and loved to talk about it. "Altogether, I am kind of glad that I made this trip because it shows me how much happier I am over there [in California], and how much I miss the American way of life."

Spain was a relief. He could conduct business, and the living style seemed more relaxed and comfortable to him. He even preferred the language to the harsh sounds of German.

His visit to Costa Rica filled him with nostalgia. He stayed with Karl Oskar and his family and spent many hours with old friends, reliving their early experiences in the country. Over Schnapps, they probably talked about their imprisonment and deportation to the United States—or did they? That subject may have been off-limits, too recent and too divisive to discuss. But Ocki must have told his brother about life in Germany, both during the war and after, and given him more details on the deaths of their youngest brother, Ülrich, and father, Max.

I suspect Ocki probably glossed over the war years, a miserable succession of days spent trying to get sufficient food and adequate shelter. But he loved telling the story about faking his way into a job that gave him steady income after the war. Years later, he told it to me with obvious glee. While trying to find transportation into Hamburg to look for work, Ocki stumbled on a U.S. soldier about to change the tire of his car. He helped out and was offered a ride. Asked about available jobs, the soldier mentioned their need for an experienced manager at a

Women's Air Corp hotel for occupying American forces. Ocki immediately claimed vast experience, demonstrated a fair command of English, and was hired.[1]

In spite of the warm welcome my father was given in Costa Rica, he found that it was no longer home. He wrote to my mother, "My wish, without question earlier, to turn right around and return, no longer exists.... my beloved California[,] Seabright and Santa Cruz is now in first place and at the front is my small sweet family."

When Werner returned, he dropped his suitcases and gave us children bear hugs, then rummaged through his luggage for a newly purchased record of Costa Rican dance music, which he immediately put on the phonograph. While he swirled our mother around the living room, we laughed and applauded. Looking back, I realize now that finally, after so many years, Papi was where he wanted to be. His exile was over, and he was home.

In the years that followed, Werner expanded his business to include wine-bottle labels, lead foil caps, and the machinery for putting the caps on the bottles. The walls of his office were papered with wine labels—his samples. Ashtrays overflowed with cigarette stubs. Always conscientious about providing for his family, my father's losses during the war years seemed to exacerbate the pressure he felt. He became driven by his work, rarely relaxing. In his last years, even brief vacations became infrequent, to Mom's sorrow and Karl's loss.

He never mentioned his experiences in World War II to Karl, Ingrid, or me, and only occasionally spoke about his youth during World War I. He died of lung cancer in 1970, barely sixty-one years old.

Mom *did* talk about the internment experience when she was pressed, but the memories overwhelmed her. Interviews in 1994, on which much of this story is based, were gathered over a period of time, piece by piece, because it was common for her to be unable to continue through her tears.

She never worked outside the home, but after Papi died, she discovered a passion for translating. For over twenty years, she voluntarily translated California's pre-statehood documents from the Spanish. All her work can be found in Special Collections, University of California at Santa Cruz.

My mother died when she was eighty-six, in 1997. *The Diary and Copybook of William E. P. Hartnell*, which she translated and Glenn J. Farris edited, was published in 2004 by the California Missions Study Association (Arthur H. Clark Company, Santa Clara, California).

Were our parents embittered by their ordeal? No, but they were wary and always alert to the possibility that what had happened to them could happen again, to themselves or to others. They appreciated the freedoms they had and never took them for granted. They voted at every election and followed national and world events with keen attention. We children learned about both the rights and the responsibilities of citizenship.

Perhaps most important, they taught us to value truth. They collected and weighed information; they probed and discussed gathered facts. They understood all too well the damage jumping to conclusions could do.

"Home at Last" Endnotes

1 For more on repatriates' experiences in Germany, see Friedman, *Nazis and Good Neighbors*, 203–9; Art Jacobs, *The Prison Called Hohenasperg: An American Boy Betrayed by His Government During World War II* (Parkland, Fla.: Universal Publishers, 1999); and Stephen Fox, *Fear Itself: Inside the FBI Roundup of German Americans during World War II* (Lincoln, Nebraska: iUniverse Inc., 2005). The German American Internee Coalition Web site, http://www.gaic.info, has a number of internee stories as well.

REUNION

In November 2002, Ingrid and I traveled back to the site of the Crystal City, Texas, family camp for the first time since we left in 1944. The trip was triggered by an invitation to a reunion of former internees, made possible by the efforts of the Zavala County Historical Commission and its able chairman, Richard Santos. The invitation coincided with Veterans' Day and the Crystal City Spinach Festival, an annual event celebrating the mainstay crop of the area. The Festival added a surreal element to the gravity of the reunion itself.

Ingi and I debated. After all, she remembered nothing of the experience, and I had only a few memories: icicles on a cracked, brown plate; brilliant lights shining through bedroom curtains; nursery-school songs; and a dust storm. What was the point of revisiting that particular place and time?

We have seventeen pictures taken by the authorities from those days: our family's "mug shot," taken for camp files—weary, blank-eyed parents still stunned by their ordeal, with solemn, watchful children; a few of the nursery school; one photo of the workers of the maintenance division; most of them of us, the children, on Christmas Eve, 1943. Looking at them again, Ingrid and I realized we had a hunger to learn more about our experiences there, so we booked the flight to Texas, hoping to find someone who would recognize our family—someone who could fill in the gaps in our history.

Purposely arriving a day early, we drove to the camp's site to check it out while we could be alone. Very little remained of the camp itself, only a few cement foundations of original bungalows and remnants of the swimming pool, partially excavated and cleaned out just for this occasion.

Maybe eventually, an accurate historical marker will be placed at the internment camp site, recognizing all the nationalities interned. A current marker, funded privately and placed in 1985, incorrectly states that only Japanese-American prisoners were held there. Mr. Santos and the historical commission hope to have the entire site recognized as a national historic park, and to that end, they have identified former bungalows sold to local residents and moved off-site. In the future, they would like to move those houses back. They are also collecting oral histories and memorabilia from internees and former camp employees, planning to build a museum there.[1]

Nothing seemed familiar in the mild light of a golden afternoon, but as we sat, Ingrid and I, on the edge of the pool our father helped to build, we could not speak for tears. The barbed-wire fence, barracks, and bungalows were gone. There were no armed prison guards in their towers, no prisoners. But the shadow of our past was there, despite the soft, green grass and gentle breeze. We were free now to walk away, but that shadow—that remembered or imagined pain—was part of the entire weekend for us and for the others who came.

Of the thousands of prisoners who passed through the camp during the war years, we were two of around eighty internees of German descent at the reunion. There was a busload of Japanese with ties to Peru and a handful of others. Most of us were the children of the camp.

We were feted at receptions and memorial services and included in the annual Spinach Festival parade as a collective grand marshal. The parade featured the Spinach Queen and her court, local school bands, floats, pickup trucks full of high-school and junior-high athletes, flag twirlers, and us. The streets were lined with onlookers, many of whom cheered as we walked by. Some were curious enough to walk along, asking us about our time at the camp or telling us about their memories of it. A small group of aging World War II veterans stood and clapped when we reached their seating area. I like to think they realized that we, too, were veterans of a sort. The statue of Popeye my parents saw as we were driven to the camp in 1943 still smoked his pipe by the downtown courthouse.

But the real story of the reunion happened over meals, in motel parking lots, in vans on the way to an event ... everywhere we gathered. All of us were searching for more information, all hoping to find someone who would recognize us and our families, all collecting shards of memories. We had the gift of sharing a common experience, and so we could share the anger, the sorrow, and the bewilderment we felt. Some were still fearful; in their past, being identified as German or as an internee had brought suffering—lost jobs, derision from neighbors, shunning by schoolmates. Many were wistful; they had nothing, not even a single photograph, to help recall their childhood. A small number were activists, campaigning to have the U.S. government acknowledge these past injustices.

Others were stoic or appeared to be. "What's past is past" seemed to be their motto. And yet one man, after dispassionately telling me a bit about his family— a terrible story of war and postwar life in Germany after years of imprisonment in the United States; of bombings, refugee camps, and stealing food to survive; of being an American enemy in Germany after being a German enemy in America—suddenly switched from a handshake to a bear hug before he turned away, shaken.

Many lost so much more than my family did. Many families were destroyed by the years of insecurity and fear. Some who were repatriated died in Russian or

German prisoner-of-war camps. Others died in the bombings or of starvation. A number simply vanished, lost forever, like the youngest brother of the Honduran man who met and eventually married my cousin, Hermida. My cousin's husband-to-be was able to escape from a train carrying prisoners in Russia by wriggling through a hole in the floorboards while the train was stopped. His sixteen-year-old brother squirmed only partially free when the train started, and he was carried away, never to be seen again.

Two women at the reunion were adults when interned. One of them knew my family—in particular, my aunt and uncle. She had lived near them in Costa Rica before the imprisonments and deportations began. Irma and her family were sent to Germany on the *Gripsholm* in the same exchange as Ocki, Pany, and Hermida, and there they met my grandparents and my youngest uncle, Üllie. Both my grandfather and Üllie died in the closing months of the war, so we children never knew them.

My sister and I left the reunion with slightly more information about our family than we had when we arrived. But the biggest lesson we learned was that our story is not unique. The number of civilians detained by the United States during WWII is staggering. The true cost of these programs comes home when one realizes that each number represents a person—a man forcibly removed from his home and business; a woman who weeps for her husband, brother, or son; a child bewildered and afraid. Herded onto trains, buses, or ships, we began our secret journeys to unseen prisons here in the United States, where the words "liberty and justice for all" ring clearly in the Pledge of Allegiance.

Judge Learned Hand once said,

> That community is already in the process of dissolution where each man begins to eye his neighbor as a possible enemy, where nonconformity with the accepted creed, political as well as religious, is a mark of disaffection; where denunciation, without specification or backing, takes the place of evidence; where orthodoxy chokes freedom of dissent; where faith in the eventual supremacy of reason has become so timid that we dare not enter our convictions in the open lists, to win or lose. (Speech, Convocation of the Board of Regents, University of the State of New York, October 24, 1952)

After the September 11, 2001 terrorist attacks on the World Trade Center and the Pentagon, concern about national security is understandable, but our fear for the future must not prevent looking at our past and tempering our actions with the truths we learn there. Neither race nor ethnicity has ever been sufficient basis to declare an entire people an enemy. Now, as in World War II, democratic ideals we cherish are damaged when we allow our government to act secretly and illegally against individuals, denying them the basic human and civil rights our Constitution guarantees.

Yesterday, my family was imprisoned. Unless we acknowledge our mistakes and somehow learn from our past, tomorrow it may be yours. Take heed.

"Reunion" Endnotes

[1] In February 2007 the Texas Historical Commission installed a marker at Crystal City that describes the ethnicity of the population held during World War II as "Japanese, German, and Italian nationals arrested in the U.S. and Hawaii, and in Peru and other Latin American countries …" The other marker remains at the site as well.

A Wider View

Why was the United States pivotal in the creation and administration of the Latin-American program? U.S. policies were motivated by three concerns: national and hemispheric security, economic rivalry for Latin-American markets, and the third, least savory purpose—gathering captives to use for barter with Axis countries holding American prisoners.[1]

National and Hemispheric Security

In 1936, the president of the United States, Franklin Delano Roosevelt, worried about the growing militancy of Germany, authorized J. Edgar Hoover, head of the Federal Bureau of Investigation, to begin a secret five-year plan. He was to identify U.S. citizens and legal residents who might pose possible future security risks. In April 1941, Hoover justified this program in a note to Attorney General Robert Jackson.

> You will recall that ... in accord with the instructions of the President the Bureau initiated a program of establishing and maintaining a list of persons whose activities were considered so dangerous as to justify consideration of their detention in the event of a national emergency ... None of these persons today has violated a specific Federal law now in force and effect, but many of them will come within the category for internment or prosecution as a result of regulations and laws which may be enacted in the event of a declaration of war. To wait until then to gather such information or to conduct such investigations would be suicidal.[2]

Attorney General Jackson responded to this declaration with a memo to all department and agency heads, including Hoover, stating, "[The FBI] cannot be used except for the investigation of crimes and subversive activities which amount to overt acts rather than matter of opinion."[3] Ignoring Jackson, Hoover secretly continued to compile his list, retitled as the Custodial Detention Index (CDI). Categorized within it were those people who should be arrested and imprisoned immediately if war broke out, as well as those to be watched carefully.

Immediately after the Japanese attack on Pearl Harbor—December 7, 1941— arrests began.

Roosevelt was also concerned that Nazi elements would become established in Central and South America and might gain the support of existing governments, many of whom he considered both politically unstable and incapable. In 1936, he began attempts to line up Latin-American republics' endorsement of an American plan that mandated compulsory consultation with the United States, if any republic were attacked by a non-hemispheric power. Not sure of cooperation from all the Latin-American republics, he issued a directive on June 26, 1939, authorizing the formation of a new secret intelligence agency to be deployed for espionage and counterespionage in Latin America.

Originally the FBI, Military Intelligence Division (MID) and the Office of Naval Intelligence (ONI) were jointly responsible for building and running the program. Faced with a power struggle among these groups, Adolf Berle, assistant secretary of state, announced at a joint meeting in June 1940 that the president had decided to give the FBI control of the new agency.[4] The Secret Intelligence Service (SIS) was officially created on July 1, 1940, by J. Edgar Hoover.

Surreptitiously, the FBI had had the first of its agents in place in Latin America by May, prior to that announcement. Their task was to compile secret lists of persons presumed to be potential threats to the United States. They were assisted by William Stephenson, a Canadian businessman selected by the British to create an agency to collect information for Great Britain and plan counter-measures to fascist and Nazi operations in the western hemisphere.

He operated out of New York, heading the British Security Coordination (BSC), which coordinated the work of British agents already in place and added to their number. Working with the FBI, he encouraged their expansion into the international arena by giving them technical assistance and helping them place their own agents in Central and South America.[5] Positioned as legal or civil attachés with consulates and embassies, or as legitimate businessmen, many were poorly trained and spoke no Spanish.

In February 1941, Assistant Secretary of State Berle wrote a State Department document, "The Pattern of Nazi Organization and Their Activities in the Other American Republics." In it, he made indiscriminate statements labeling many German groups as subversive, indicting German commercial firms as "indispensable media for the operation of the Nazi system," and asserting that "… virtually all the Reichsdeutschen [Germans born in Germany] in Latin America are sincere supporters of the Nazi regime" and "virtually every non-Jewish German citizen belongs to some branch of the Nazi hierarchy." He called for all ambassadorial and consular officers to report any suspicious Germans and activities of German commercial firms.[6]

Coded as strictly confidential, the document was sent to Latin-American embassies, and soon reports came pouring in of people "believed to possess Nazi sympathies" from "sources generally considered reliable." The stage was set for the sweeping arrests and imprisonments that followed.[7]

Meanwhile, the FBI and ONI continued wrangling over who should run the SIS, until Roosevelt, in April 1941, proposed a new "coordinator of information" for the western hemisphere, Col. William J. Donovan. When Col. Donovan was confirmed in July, he began work to create one, centralized intelligence service, the Office of Strategic Services (OSS), and was supported in his efforts by Stephenson, his British counterpart. The Latin-American section of the OSS immediately began investigating the level and commitment of pro-Nazi forces. The resultant reports indicated some potential Axis support in most Latin-American and Caribbean countries.

Also in 1941, the administration successfully sought the passage of a Lend-Lease Act, permitting the president to loan or lease supplies to nations whose defense was considered vital to the United States. Originally this allowed the supply of war materials to England. Later provisions extended lend-lease arrangements to Latin-American republics, authorizing the sale of surplus defense and antiaircraft equipment, if the countries agreed to U.S. demands for detention and deportation of ethnic Italians, Germans, and Japanese within their borders and the expropriation of their assets.

Hoover fought vigorously to prevent OSS usurpation of his agency's authority in Latin America, and by January 1942, FDR ordered Col. Donovan to keep his OSS agents north of the Rio Grande.[8] It was not until 1945 that FBI control of Latin-American intelligence activities was turned over to the OSS successor, the Central Intelligence Group, later to become the Central Intelligence Agency.

On the diplomatic front, Army and Navy officers were secretly sent to nineteen Latin-American countries in June 1940 to negotiate agreements for defense of the western hemisphere. Negotiations concluded in October without agreements from all the countries.

A conference of western-hemisphere countries met in Rio de Janeiro January 15–28, 1942. By then, most Latin-American republics had severed Axis diplomatic ties or entered war on the Allied side. At the insistence of the United States, an Emergency Advisory Committee for Political Defense was created to monitor "alien enemies" in Latin America, requiring registration, increasing surveillance, limiting internal travel, and forbidding aliens to have guns and transmitters (though radios without transmitting capacities were also seized)—the same restrictions then in place in the United States. Naturalization procedures were to be slowed, so aliens could not become citizens. Detention was urged and cancellation of citizenship was recommended for any native-born or naturalized citizen who supported the Axis powers in any way.[9] The first arrests and deportations quietly began.[10]

By November 1942, a secret memo detailing the work being done to remove aliens was written and distributed to all U.S. diplomatic posts in Latin America. Since "all German nationals without exception, all Japanese nationals, a small proportion of Italian nationals, and more individuals than might be expected among the political and racial refugees from Central Europe are all dangerous," methods that might be used to increase the numbers being deported were suggested.

The author also noted a change in policy. The United States originally deported only males, leaving women and children behind. But this procedure had failed, since the families, left without means, complained to local authorities and "have become a very dangerous focus of anti-United States propaganda." The new recommendation was to deport everyone in the family.[11]

In 1943, in Montevideo, the Emergency Advisory Committee adopted U.S. Department of Justice/State Department resolutions to allow the United States to provide detention accommodations and shipping expenses for Latin Axis nationals to the United States, a process already under way for the past eighteen months.

Under intense pressure from the United States, eighteen Latin-American countries, many of them smaller countries in the Caribbean area and the northern part of South America, took advantage of U.S. willingness to subsidize the imprisonment and deportation program. Mexico, Venezuela, and Brazil began internment programs of their own, while Chile, attempting to stay neutral, used its own legal system to deal with Germans considered a threat. All four countries eventually allowed deportation of some Axis nationals to the U.S. Germans residing in Argentina remained largely untouched, because the government tended to be pro-fascist.[12]

Was the administration right to be so concerned about Nazi infiltration in Latin America? Fears that Germany might seize power in some Latin-American countries and then stage incursions into the United States were not unrealistic. Germany was a strong, militant country rapidly annexing new territories by force, and reports from the OSS, FBI, and BSC all indicated at least some level of Nazi activity in Latin America. For national security, continued U.S. control of the Panama Canal was essential, since it provided convenient passage between the Atlantic and Pacific oceans, where the United States was fighting simultaneous battles.

Certainly, many of the German Latin Americans were linked by culture, family, and affection to their motherland. Some were generally supportive of the increasingly militaristic stance taken by Germany, while others became vociferous exponents. But most were Latin Americans first and foremost, no matter what their citizenship. Far from their birthplaces, they had made homes in their countries of choice, and that was where their true loyalty lay.

Realistic evaluation of the potential threat posed by fascist efforts in Latin America was hampered by inaccurate and sometimes intentionally misleading reports and news stories. Agents sent to collect information were often poorly trained and unable to speak either German or Spanish. Histrionic claims were produced (and believed by some) that all Germans residing in Latin America actively supported Hitler's policies. United States officials made the erroneous assumption that ethnicity alone decided loyalty. Once that assumption was in place, all Germans became the enemy.

In Rout's and Bratzel's *The Shadow War,* the authors discuss German intelligence in Latin America, with detailed information about espionage and counterespionage efforts in four countries: Mexico, Brazil, Argentina, and Chile. They conclude, "In essence, the German intelligence apparatus in Latin America was both hastily built and poorly developed" (18). They estimate there were only about five hundred Axis agents in place throughout the Americas. Of the more than four thousand Germans deported from Latin America to internment camps in the United States, assertions of espionage were leveled against only eight, and no one was ever brought to trial.[13]

Economic Considerations

Military security was not the only United States motive for increasing intervention in Central and South America. Control of Axis-owned businesses was desirable to block the possible use of their profits for Nazi support, but another aim was to eliminate competition with United States companies. Covert United States arrangements with some countries led to the removal of the German management and personnel of airlines in Colombia in 1939, and in Ecuador, Bolivia, and Chile over the next few years ... and the subsequent rise of United States companies to fill the gaps.[14]

Following the lead of the British, who published an economic blacklist in August 1940, the State Department, in June 1941, ordered its delegations in Latin America to gather information for similar restrictions by the United States. Franklin Delano Roosevelt's Proclamation 2497 on July 17, 1941, declared the Proclaimed List of Certain Blocked Nationals—people and businesses whom the United States would no longer deal with economically. This effectively prevented any company from dealing with them, since it would be placed on the list itself if it did so.[15]

In Costa Rica, the government created the Oficina de Coordinación (Coordinating Office) in October 1941, an agency to oversee the agricultural and industrial businesses of those on the Proclaimed List. By doing so, they hoped to ensure that production continued, benefiting Costa Rican workers, but that profits were funneled into frozen accounts, preventing them from being used for Axis goals. The program was so successful that other Central American countries copied it, hoping to support the economic boycott without damaging their own economies.

In spite of the program's success, another organization with expanded powers was substituted on March 25, 1942, largely due to the insistence of the United States. The new organization was named the Junta de Custodia de la Propiedad de los Nacionales de los Países en Guerra con Costa Rica (Custodial Board of the Property of Nationals from Countries at War with Costa Rica) or Junta de Custodia de la Propiedad Enemiga (Enemy Property Custodial Board). Known as the Junta de Custodia, it had vastly expanded powers against Axis citizens on the Proclaimed List. It was able to levy taxes on their frozen funds, to expropriate, and—if desired—sell all assets it felt necessary for defense purposes, and to demand extra duties or tributes before allowing enemy aliens any access to their accounts. Many of the board's decisions were influenced or demanded by the United States.

The moneys made from sales of expropriated properties were deposited in government coffers, while government-issued bonds were placed in the frozen accounts. These bonds paid an annual interest rate far less than the amount of tax levied yearly. By 1945, the government of Costa Rica, badly in debt, began raiding the remaining frozen funds as an emergency loan to support itself. The money was soon exhausted.[16]

Bargaining Chips

The third motive was clearly stated in an internal State Department memo in November 1942. The "Nations of Central America and the Caribbean islands [sic] have in general been willing to send us subversive aliens without placing any limitation on our disposition of them. In other words, we could repatriate them, we could intern them or we could hold them in escrow for bargaining purposes." It went on: "It is particularly desirable that the repatriation of inherently harmless Axis nationals may be used to the greatest possible extent" to obtain release of Allied citizens in Axis countries.[17] "Inherently harmless" people being imprisoned and exchanged clearly demonstrates that the U.S. motive was not only security of the western hemisphere.

Most people now agree that United States' measures against perceived enemies were much too sweeping in the Second World War, broadly targeting certain ethnic groups without adequate proof of guilt. Commissions have already judged as misguided and racist the Japanese-American and Latin-American detention programs. In November 2000, the Wartime Violations of Italian American Civil Liberties Act recognized the government's wrongful denial of Italian-American civil liberties. The Wartime Treatment Study Act, designed to create the first independent review and evaluation of United States WWII policies directed against other European ethnic groups within the United States and in Latin America, has been introduced in every Congress since 2001. It has not been acted on.

"A Wider View" Endnotes

[1] Krammer, *Undue Process,* 91–92; see also Barnhart, "Japanese Internees," 171; Max Paul Friedman, "Specter of a Nazi Threat: United States-Colombian Relations, 1939–1945," *The Americas,* April 2000.

[2] J. Edgar Hoover, memo to Attorney General Robert Jackson, 1 April 1941, *From the Secret Files of J. Edgar Hoover,* edited with commentary by Athan Theoharis (Chicago: Ivan R. Dee, 1991), 187, 190.

[3] Attorney General Robert Jackson, memo to all department and agency heads, undated but circa April 1941, *From the Secret Files of J. Edgar Hoover,* 185.

[4] Leslie B. Rout Jr. and John F. Bratzel, *The Shadow War: German Espionage and United States Counterespionage in Latin America During World War II* (Maryland: University Publications of America, 1986), 28; see also Jerre Mangione, *An Ethnic at Large: A Memoir of America in the Thirties and Forties* (New York: G.P. Putnam's Sons, 1978), 282.

[5] See Rout and Bratzel, *Shadow War* and Mangione, *Ethnic at Large,* for more.

[6] Adolf Berle, memo to chiefs of the diplomatic missions in the other American republics, "The Pattern of Nazi Organization and Their Activities in the Other American Republics," 6 February 1941, decimal file 862.20210/414A, 250/34/7/4, Box 5505, RG 59, NA.

[7] Rout and Bratzel, *Shadow War,* 12.

[8] Rout and Bratzel, *Shadow War,* 37.

[9] Krammer, *Undue Process,* 92–93.

[10] Friedman, *Nazis and Good Neighbors,* 120–22; see also Krammer, *Undue Process,* 92; and Barnhart, "Japanese Internees."

[11] "Memorandum Regarding the Activities of the United States Government in Removing from the Other American Republics Dangerous Subversive Aliens," 3 November 1942, 3, RG 59, Subject Files, Box 180, location 250/49/7, Records of the Special War Problems Division, NA.

[12] White to Lafoon, 30 January 1946, "Statistics," Box 70, Special War Problems Division, R.G 59 NA and Friedman, *Nazis and Good Neighbors,* 9.

[13] Friedman, *Nazis and Good Neighbors,* 9.

[14] Friedman, *Nazis and Good Neighbors,* 106–107; see also Krammer, *Undue Process,* 92; and Friedman, "Specter of a Nazi Threat," 566–67.

[15] Friedman, "Specter of a Nazi Threat," 575.

16 Carlos Calvo Gamboa, *Costa Rica en la Segunda Guerra Mundial* (1939–45), 44–45, and Friedman, *Nazis and Good Neighbors*, 171–76.

17 "Memorandum Regarding the Activities of the United States Government in Removing from the Other American Republics Dangerous Subversive Aliens," 3 November 1942; also, Friedman, *Nazis and Good Neighbors*, 199–200.

SELECTED BIBLIOGRAPHY

Alien Enemy Detention Facility, Immigration and Naturalization Service, 1946. 16 mm videocassette, N3-85-86-1, National Archives (N.A.), College Park, Maryland.

Barnhart, Edward N. "Japanese Internees from Peru." *Pacific Historical Review* 31 (1962).

Berle, Adolf. Memo to chiefs of the diplomatic missions in the other American republics, "The Pattern of Nazi Organization and Their Activities in the Other American Republics." 6 February 1941, Decimal File 862.20210/414A, 250/34/7/4, Box 5505, RG 59, NA.

Biddle, Francis. *In Brief Authority.* New York: Doubleday and Company Inc., 1962.

Calvo Gamboa, Carlos. *Costa Rica en la Segunda Guerra Mundial (1939–1945).* San José, Costa Rica: Editorial Universidad Estatal a Distancia, 1985.

Christgau, John. *Enemies.* Lincoln, Nebraska: iUniverse Inc., 2001. (Reprint of *Enemies: World War II Alien Internment.* Ames: Iowa State University Press, 1985.)

Commission on Wartime Relocation and Internment of Civilians. *Personal Justice Denied.* Seattle: The Civil Liberties Public Education Fund and the University of Washington Press, 1997.

Distasi, Lawrence, ed. *Una Storia Segreta.* Berkeley: Heyday Books, 2001.

Emmerson, John K. *The Japanese Thread: A Life in the U.S. Foreign Service.* New York: Holt, Rinehart, and Winston, 1978.

Fiset, Louis. "Medical Care for Interned Enemy Aliens: a Role for the US Health Service in World War II," *American Journal of Public Health*, 2003 October; 93 (10): 1644–1654. http://www.pubmedcentral.nih.gov/articlerender.fcgi?artid=1448029

Fox, Stephen. *Fear Itself: Inside the FBI Roundup of German Americans during World War II*. Lincoln, Nebraska: iUniverse Inc., 2005.

——. "The Deportation of Latin American Germans, 1941–47: Fresh Legs for Mr. Monroe's Doctrine." *Yearbook of German-American Studies* 32 (1997).

Friedman, Max Paul. *Nazis and Good Neighbors: The United States Campaign Against the Germans of Latin America in World War II*. New York: Cambridge University Press, 2003.

——. "Specter of a Nazi Threat: United States-Columbian Relations, 1939–1945." *The Americas* (April 2000).

——. "Private Memory, Public Record, and Contested Terrain: Weighing Oral Testimony in the Deportation of Germans from Latin America During World War II," *Oral History Review* 27/1 (Winter/Spring 2000).

Gardiner, C. Harvey. *Pawns in a Triangle of Hate: The Peruvian Japanese and the United States*. Seattle: University of Washington Press, 1981.

German American Internee Coalition Web site: http://www.gaic.info

Goodwin, Doris Kearns. *No Ordinary Time. Franklin and Eleanor Roosevelt: The Home Front in World War II*. New York: Simon and Schuster, 1994.

Guerrero Portales, Rudy. *Costa Rica y Los Estados Unidos en la Segunda Guerra Mundial*. San José, Costa Rica: Editorial Costa Rica, 1944.

Haagen, Paul H. "A Hamburg Childhood: The Early Life of Herbert Bernstein." *Duke Journal of Comparative & International Law* 13: no. 3, p. 7, summer 2003 (http://ssrn.com/abstract=460201).

Hyde, H. Montgomery. *Room 3603*. New York: Farrar, Straus, and Company, 1963.

Jacobs, Arthur. *The Prison Called Hohenasperg: An American Boy Betrayed by His Government During World War II.* Parkland, Florida: Universal Publishers, 1999.

———. "Internment of German Americans in the United States during World War II." The *Freedom of Information Times*, http://www.foitimes.com.

Kashima, Tetsuden. *Judgment Without Trial: Japanese American Imprisonment During World War II.* Seattle: University of Washington Press, 2003.

Kimball, Warren F. *The Most Unsordid Act: Lend-Lease, 1939–1941.* Baltimore: John Hopkins Press, 1969.

Kogawa, Joy. *Obasan.* New York: Doubleday, 1994.

Krammer, Arnold. *Undue Process: The Untold Story of America's German Alien Internees.* Maryland: Rowman and Littlefield Publishers Inc., 1997.

Lefever, Ernest W. *Ethics and United States Foreign Policy.* New York: Meridian Books Inc., 1957.

Mangione, Jerre G. *An Ethnic at Large: A Memoir of America in the Thirties and Forties.* New York: G. P. Putnam's Sons, 1978.

"Memorandum Regarding the Activities of the United States Government in Removing from the Other American Republics Dangerous Subversive Aliens," 3 November 1942, 3, RG 59, Subject Files, Box 180, location 250/49/7, Records of the Special War Problems Division, NA.

O'Rourke, Joseph L. *Historical Narrative of the Crystal City Internment Camp*, a report to W. F. Kelly, assistant commissioner for Alien Control, Immigration and Naturalization Service, Crystal City Internment Camp, RG 85, 101/161, 32, NA.

Rout, Jr., Leslie B., and John F. Bratzel. *The Shadow War: German Espionage and United States Counterespionage in Latin America During World War II.* Frederick, Maryland: University Publications of America Inc., 1986.

Theoharis, Athan G., and John Stuart Cox. *The Boss: J. Edgar Hoover and the Great American Inquisition.* Philadelphia: Temple University Press, 1988.

Theohari, Athan G., ed. *From the Secret Files of J. Edgar Hoover*. Chicago: Ivan R. Dee, 1991.

Thompson, Lea. *Roundup*. Produced by Chris Scholl. Dateline NBC, 30 November 1994.

United States Department of Justice. "Regulations Controlling Travel and Other Conduct of Aliens of Enemy Nationalities," United States Government Printing Office, Washington, 1942.

Weglyn, Michi Nishiura. *Years of Infamy: The Untold Story of America's Concentration Camps*. Seattle: University of Washington Press, 1996.

978-0-595-39333-6
0-595-39333-0

Printed in the United States
201810BV00002B/1-105/P